ASSORTED FEELINGS

ABBAS MEHDI

BlueRose Publishers
New Delhi • London

First Published in October 2021
ISBN: 978-93-5472-482-4

BLUEROSE PUBLISHERS
www.bluerosepublishers.com
info@bluerosepublishers.com
+91 8882 898 898
Cover Design:
Muskan Sachdeva
Typographic Design:
Ilma Mirza

Distributed by: BlueRose, Amazon, Flipkart

INDEX

A BACKDROP ON THE CONCEPT

Right from the age of 18 that is my college days I had a strong desire to write which urged me to set sail on my penning journey with poetry to start with in the 70" till I realized graduation that all my life I could not to be dreamer or Nightingale sitting in the dark to jeer solitude with sweet sounds!

Hence, now confined to reality and the struggle for a decent living, I would only write occasionally when really inspired on topics which touched the very core of my heart and preserved them over the years, never-the-less on reviewing my above mentioned journey and collection at this stage of my life of the last 30 years, I realized that there were enough topics or issues on which I had written something which could be compiled in to – a book.

Initially, I thought of sharing only my real life experiences of true happening or unforgettable experiences in the form of short unusual stories but since I had written a few poems, I thought of adding a little of my inner self believing it would add a different flavor and cater to a larger audience.

However, on discussing concept with my wife I was advised by her to include some of my published letters to the press on the socio, economic & political trend of the last few year when, I was asked by another of my friend why not to add a few of your jottings and unpublished letter to give vent to some of your un-attended gut feelings which need to be addressed by those concerned.

In short, the book I desire to publish is a mix of my very TRUE and REAL emotions with not a pinch of fiction, hence the title "Assorted feelings." Which I hope will make it something different.

A PERFACE

The life of every individual is characterized by certain events or moments which become unforgettable some may be very humorous, a few sad another few inspiring and educative leaving an everlasting impression in your memory which is generally stored in the hard disk of the human computer and appears on the mental screen in a flash when recalled.

As an individual I have had my share of a number of unforgettable days and events which I have tried to recollect as vividly as possible from my memory land and pen down, in doling so each event seemed to become a small story which I wish to share at large inducing sometimes a laughter, a tear, or a lesson or an inspiration or just an unexpected or unusual episode at times.

MY MOTHER

The one who cares for me on earth,

She is the one, who gave me birth,

To see me in grief, she can never bear,

My sorrows she always wants to share.

As a baby when, I had learnt to talk,

She held my hand and taught me to walk,

When I was four, I remember well,

The fairy tales, to me, she would tell,

Whenever she has seen me sad,

She wants to know what troubles I had,

But when to her my joys, I tell,

Happy for me, I saw she felt.

Though from her I live miles apart,

Her thoughts forever, stay in my heart,

To play with her my heart it wills,

And wants to be a baby still.

My love for her I cannot speak

Words in her praise, I have yet to seek,

A Goddess, I adore and pray,

And shall love her till my dying day.

Dedicated To My Mother

A.G. Mehdi

DREAMS ARE ALL I HAVE

Of Diamonds, Rubies, Pears and all the precious stones,

If I were not poor, all alone ....

A dress I would make of them for you to wear.

But my dreams are all I have,

For you to share.

My dreams more precious than all the stones,

Yes, on your path I spread my dreams alone,

None other shall have them for they are rare,

Do not crush them, oh, please step with care!

REALITY A DESPAIR

Now those dreams are no more for you,

Nor the love (for you) I bore,

My desires, my pride with your artfulness you slew,

You angel! Will you be loved ever more?

Gone, gone to the winds this flowery romance,

What use now of pretense..........

You are a goddess of no romance,

Of it I live no more in ignorance.'

A.G. Mehdi

AIMLESSLY

At parting day ....

I in solitude down and low.

Walk aimlessly to reach the beach,

Retrospecting, feeling choked with despair.

As I stand at the lands end

I watch the waves rollover

And perceive only question

To which I have answers none.

A huge wave dashes against a rock,

And haunts my mind tormenting my very soul.

I still keep standing ....

Gazing at the oblivious horizon endlessly,

A serine softness, gradually

Engulfs the harsh din within me,

I then sit aloof and alone watching

Children playing, trees swaying,

Waves lapping, people returning

And sweet adieus.

The cool breeze, pulverizes,

Caresses and chills me.

A tear eye to mouth,

I get up and start walking

Aimlessly with a saline test

On my tongue!

A.G. Mehdi

DREAM AND REALITY

O heart of mine

Is there a place

A place, sweet and lovely

Where twilight dwells

And love abides

In which I can be lost?

Sweet sleep comes then

To take me in her lap.

The world for me searches

But I am nowhere to be found.

In a dream

My dream I meet

Sing then to her

My once a love untold

She smiles at me

For hours we speak

Love fragrances blows

A fulfillment reached.

Says then a voice

"Shall I leave "?

With a broken dream

Far from my world

I find myself in reality

Harsh, cold and ugly.

A.G. Mehdi.

THE RARE OCCASION

Life full of restrictions, bars,

Suppressions and limitations ,

Of feelings and desires ....

Desires to express emotions

Buried deep in silience

A silience that speaks .

The spring of disenchantment ....

Finally finds its way .....

To join the stream of tears

A sprinkling of salt ......

On wounds unseen.

A time of strife

Finds a forsaken

On a path lonely

Dazed ....

At the desertion

Of even his shadow !

Uncomprehendable life

In sadness a foe

A friend of happiness

Happiness the rare occasion .

A.G. Mehdi .

TODAY ' S JUDGMENT

In the criminal box stood mighty riches

In the witness, miserably exploited poverty

Stood then the criminal amongst hapless people .

The suppressed witness swore though on books holy ,

Were forced to built a tale of lies colossal

Pathetic it seemed to witness those

Disgusting scenes of humiliating aversion

Poverty – gloomy, frustrated and desperate,

Exhibited its accentuated weakness

Contrary riches stood sneering mocking and defiant

As exemplary of falsification personified.

'Benefit of the Doubt" granted to the accused

Proclaimed the judge,

Got away the arrogant ....

With deceit in cold blood.

Today's judgment ....

A verdict in favors of Riches!

A.G. Mehdi

TO MY LOVE

Love has made me I know not what

Pray hark, should I love there or not?

Let it be not, that if I should stumble and fall

I find not your arms to lift me

And I to nothingness be turned

If you do not render ....

The touch of your loving love.

You are the life of my dreams

But have I ever walked in your dreams?

Do ask your loving eyes

To assure me a dawn

In the darkness of my nights.

A.G. Mehdi

PRINCIPLES FORGOTTEN?

Oh! Ahmedabad

Oh! Thirsty soil of Ahmedabad

Have you quenched your thirst?

Alas, it was a scene

I could not bear to see

So full of grief and pain

As I passed its many

Abandoned lonely streets

Just yesterday which was bustling

With peace loving people

What flooded Sabarmati?

The Sabarmati, on the banks of which,

The father of the nation

Once preached non-violence

Equality and human brotherhood

There, now, might was right

For we are Hindus and they are Muslims,

They love Mohammed and we love Ram,

But we loved not the principles preached,

In the Gita or the Koran,

And so one followed his "dharma"

The other his "mazhab"

But can the heart of so great a mystery

Be reached by one path only?

God is one – The only Father

So, one stoned his house

The other pulled it down

Oh! Ahmedabad are we not brothers,

Or is the religion of Humanity forgotten?

In the land of the Mahatma??

A.G. Mehdi

ON LOVE

A state of mind

A concept of being

A thought to care

Expressed in words or action

A sympathetic attitude

A desire to give

A sacrifice

A feeling – emotion, admiration

An advantage foregone

A wrong forgiven

A mutual respect

A wanting to be wanted

A tender touch

A word of praise

An understanding

A fulfillment

A relationship of

A mother, sister or spouse

Extremely sacred and pure

A worship

An agony untold

An ecstasy unknown

An endless chain

An infinite existence

Is love ……………..

I know not

Yes, I know

It is perennial

Or is it not ?

A.G. Mehdi

I SEEK

An endless search

To Find ....

Only foot prints

A proof of existence

But in person

Yet to meet

Echoes of silence

Echoes now returning

From comers ....

Of lands unknown

But of you no trace

Only a hazy conception

The agonized wanderings

Struggle yet not without hope

Yes Hoping, to meet, one day

The only one, I seeked .

(Dedicated to my wife as I wrote

it much before I met her.)

A DREAM

I find myself in a place beautiful

A heaven on earth so wonderful

With you alone and all snow

A better place I have yet to know

I look at the mountain peaks

Which with clouds play hide and seek,

But we hand in hand walk,

Tranquility wishes not to be broker by talk

Just then a thunder storm screams

A song of hate it seems

I lose your hand. I feel weak

My eyes close I fall on my knees

 O Dream of my dreams where art thee?

The eyes that adore thee open to see

My lips murmur your name

Dream it was, a dream in vain.

POETRY AT NIGHT

A) Darkness serenity
   A luminous room
   Humming monotony
   A cold whistle
   Some rattling sound
   A roar through the sky
   The cricket sings !

B) Low Whispers
   Faint footsteps
   Clattering glasses
   jerking laughter
   Painful moans
   Revengeful barks
   Sweet adieus
   A lamp extinguished.
   Darkness prevails.

C) A huge desk
   A creative mind
   A piece of paper
   Graceful fingers
   (Une Belle Plume)
   Satisfaction
   A fulfillment
   A verse born

LOVE

Love – a sympathetic attitude

A feeling ------ emotion

Abstract admiration

A concept of being

A state of mind

A thought of care

Expressed in words

Actions or

A desire

more to give

A sacrifice

An advantage ----

Foregone

A wrong forgiven

A mutual respect

Yet sense of wanting

Wanting to be wanted

More a sweet pain

A tender touch

A word of praise

An understanding

A madness

A innocence

A fulfillment

An endless chain

A infinite existence

Is Love

I know not

Yet I know -----

It is as perennial -----

Or is it not!

LINES TO MY BEST FRIEND

Will you be my friend

But ----

Friendship what really is it?

A rapport established

Between two beings

A peak of understanding

A height of selflessness

A degree of sympathy

A desire to share

A sense to care

A level of equality

Or just a gesture

That communicates volumes

It is ------ It is

This all

And feelings true

Great to posses

Oh ! my friend

But one, I have

He is my best

I know not how

He will accept !

You will

Will you not ?

My gratefulness

To express

I dedicate

To him

These lines

In all earnestness

Dedicate to Naushad Ginwalla

OUR WORLD

Circles smoking

Haziness of nothing

Painful lingering

Continues world.

Brothers ----------

Loving hearts

worn wickedness

poor world.

Thoughts ....

Hatred, misery

Poverty – sufferings

Sinful world.

Ecstasy – laughter

Agonized tears

Peace in war

Old world

I await

Dreams of sleep

Tomorrow's nightmare

our world. (29th April 1970)

A DREAM EVENING

For homeward bound is the busy bee

As the sun gracefully settles into the sea,

The birds bid farewell to the parting day,

The twilight stretches far across the bay ,

And blows now a cool gentle breeze

Din to tranquility gives way and has ceased

I see a scene of beauty so serene

Ah ! peace ! I could not help but dream!

Thus said to me that evening air

I have played though your beloved's hair

And for so sweet a fragrance

She seemed to be in my presence.

With all sweet names, though her I called

To her they did no justice at all

It sounded shallow my speech

To vent my feelings, alas too weak!

Then to her my love I confessed

And said Thou art to me most dearest'

Neither age no circumstances, or time

Will diminish this love of mine

Then all was lost to oblivion

Her sight, the scene and the fragrance

Dream they are called not reality

For they screen the world's sad satiety

TO THE PEOCOCK

Hark Oh ! most beauteous bird

You are king of birds in heaven and earth

Your crown gives you, your stately grace

And to you I sing a song of praise.

Your precious eyes are bright,

You give me to me a rare delight,

Fair one, twilight robes you wear

Your magnificence on earth none shares

At dawn a melodious song you sing

From trees to roof tops you wing

Your lips announce the brake of day

At evenings, a sweet adieu I hear you say.

When you walk, a walk so agile

 I watch you not for just awhile

When you stand, amidst blooming flowers

It appears there then beauty showers.

Bird at times you weep at heart

For from heaven you did, part,

But a beauty so sweet is thine

Be not sad, you are yet Devine.

Dedicated to the National

Bird of India.

DREAM

I find my self in a place beautiful

A heaven on earth so wonderful

With you alone, and all snow

A better place I have yet to know.

I look at the mountain peaks

Which with clouds play hide and seek.

But we hand in had walk,

Tranquility wishes not to broken by talk

Just then a thunder storm screams

A song that of hate it seems.

I lose your hand, I feel weak

My eyes close I fall on my knees

O ! Dream of my dream where art Thee ?

The eyes that adore thee open to see …

My lips murmur your name,

Dream It was, a dream in vain.

AT FIRST SIGHT !

At the door of my class room, I stood

There, good lord beautiful, a girl beautiful appeared,

Like others and all at her I looked,

In the heart of mine, said a voice 'O' Dear !

Beauty and sweetness she possessed

But never her eyes I had seen before

To Dilip I remarked she is best maiden,

Here I had seen for sure !

At me she stared and walked with grace

Her chin held high, with steps straight

But turned her gaze for the smile on my face.

Snatched she my heart, It was too late

Who can she be ?

Smiled Dilip at me, and asked me why?

He knew not her , but who was she ?

And all this while, where was I ?

End it is not for we crossed again.

In her deep dark eyes

I dared to gaze

She wandered why and looked amazed ?

When she came close

An effort to speak, I made in vain

No words came out

Though my lips shook.

Lamenting I stood, for she was gone

An abrupt ending to a happy song.

DISAPPOINTMENT

At her place she said on the 22nd we would meet,

Ah ! A day with her the thought was sweet

At ten that morning a phone call I made

Yes, dear she answered, and cancelled the date

but listen but I ------

She cut me short and told me why.

The vacation began I had to go to cambay

She promised to write while I was away.

No sooner I reached I posted her mail

But received no reply my hopes failed

Yet in the post, no letter with my name

A long time but none came.

Often I thought that she is lazy

My letter she has not received may be?

I couldn't get her out of my mind

Her thoughts began to blow my mind

Day and night my heart it pained

I awaited her letter but all in vain.

FROM MY DOOR STEPS

The day was bright

The weather was gay

The world smiled

What a happy day.

In the far distance

A bird was singing,

Singing to its love

Which above was wining.

The Atmosphere

Sweet and serene

The peace one earth

As in heaven seemed.

It was part of the world

A world so fair

OH! Beauteous world

But no tome to stare.

OCTOBER VACATIONS

IN THE MORNING I get up my chickens I feed

The papers then I take up to read.

Three miles a day we have started to run

Thirty minutes it takes and a lot of fun

A straight run it is, not many bends

Horse tired we are at its end.

Run, oh no I not only run

Sometimes I do bathe in the sun

Shooting we have gone for ducks

But have been out of luck

Some poems too I have composed

But hopeless ones they are, I suppose

French oh ! Yes, I have brought those books

They make me anguished in one very look

Like a horse too I often eat.

In the afternoon after lunch I sleep

Get up go out return and eat

Night it is now time to sleep

AN INCIDENT

To pass me journeys time

When I boarded the Gujarat Mail,

And not to let it pass in vain

A few verses and rhymes I lined.

My compartments cabin was empty

There was no one there

An incident very witty

If to hear you care.

The train started I settled

The rails too now rattled,

A call to the toilet I had to make

Believe me, I do not fake.

The toilet was dark

The train caught speed

My hand then parked

To do the foolish deed.

'Oh No' I had pulled the wrong chain

It was "To stop train pull chain"

I shattered, I shivered, my self I cursed

Where now to hide I thought at first.

The train stopped

I climbed the berth at the top.

The guard to the cabin came to inquire

As explanation was all that he required

Who pulled the chain ? Asked the stem faced

I presented an innocent front and looked amazed.

"It was the stop signal I suppose"

A foolish look his face did show.

He turned on his heels, walked out of the compartment,

What kind of people do the employ in this department ?

ON A CAMP COT

To fall sick is an awful thing

When on a camp cot it makes you sick

Counted ten on a boxing floor

You fill worse than a bloody wild bore

To feel better is an effort in vain

(for) invaded you are with killing pain.

No Doctor, no medicine in this a place

Though yours may be a serious case.

Cut food, smoking and your berverlies

If from fever you wish to be free.

Disgusted though, you feel not at ease

But the best thing for you is to sleep.

BE A TRUTHFUL AND OPEN MAN (IN LIFE)

My father was a very simple and honest person, worked as the Estate Manager of the Nawab Saheb of Khambhat and also happened to be his maternal cousin by virtue of which he was educated at Shivaji military school Pune and because of which when I was growing up groomed at the Royal residence of the Nawab Saheb at Bombay by sending me to St. Andrews high school Bandra and subsequently asked to pursue Bachelor's degree in Arts at St. Xavier's college Bombay.

It was in the 1st year of college perhaps 20 years of age then that I developed the habit of smoking a cigarettes occasionally, hence when I came down to Cambay /Khambhat to spend my Diwali vacations with my parents I on the sly carried a packet of cigarettes and a matchbox to smoke quietly at the back of my parents on unpacking my suitcase when confronted with my precious sly possession I became anxious and hastened to hid my cigarettes from my Father, just then I came across a shoebox in the bathroom which contained a tin of shoepolish and a brush which my army schooled father who polished his own shoes whenever he happened to call on the district collector or some government dignitary while attending to his official commitments as the caretaker of the huge estate of Nawab Saheb at Khambhat.

The initial days to my vacations passed off happily smoking in the bathroom without the slightest hint to my parents about it, however in the midst of the vacation I was invited to spend a day at one of my uncles and so I pushed off merrily in the morning only to return home after evening.

On returning home I noticed my father quite formally dressed sitting in the room having returned from one of his visits to the district collector, giving an account of his interactions with government officials was his habit generally bragging how he had impressed them, just then he wanted to use the bathroom got up and went towards it then held back and returned as if reminded of something and addressed me politely at first "Abbas do you smoke?" No Daddy, I said then a little sternly "Abbas do you smoke??" No Daddy, then a third time harshly "Abbas do you smoke???" Yes Daddy, I replied for I knew the cat was out of the bag, he must have opened the shoebox to polish his shoes for the visit to the collector!

He then added "understand one thing very clearly if you have started smoking, I would have appreciated if you would have informed us about it directly for I will feel greatly offended when a 3rd person comes and tells me that do you know your son has started smoking? besides the pocket money which we give you is meant to meet your necessary college expenses and not for blowing away in smoke, when you start earning please buy your own cigarettes and smoke openly not in bathroom!

From the very next day I quit smoking till I took up a part-time job and earned my first remuneration after which I jokingly asked him on phone, can I smoke now to which he amusingly replied, No, not in the bathroom!

This was perhaps a very clear lesson he taught me perhaps, to be a man and face the world and do things which are right hence openly! it was at the same time a lesson for me to realize the value of one's hard earned money which should not be blown up on leisure. Looking back I realize today how much his advice influenced me in molding my character and attitude in life in the years to come.

A WORTHY TRIBUTE TO MY FATHER

It was again one of the summer vacations during my college tenure that I had come down to Cambay to spend my holidays with my parents. My father being the Estate Manager of the Nawab Saheb was provided residential quarters in the huge palace premises itself thereby being available to all concerned any time of the day hence he would jokingly remark "I am on duty 24 hours of the day to the Royal family of Nawab Saheb"

The main palace building of Cambay (Khambhat) is surrounded by a boundary wall which in turn is then surrounded on 3 sides by huge open space of land with barbed wire fencing around it, just opposite the palace divided by the Municipal road which passes in between a sprawling semi slum dwelling had crept up gradually inhabited by Waghris called the Waghriwad of Khambhat. The waghris perhaps an ancient nomadic tribe have become backward due to lack of education and upliftment and are generally employed on daily wages as farm laborers or gardeners, chaukidars etc. thereby being unemployed for a greater part of the year they easily fall into the habit if stealing and buglery.

However, on an extremely hot afternoon in the moth of May when the mercury keeps rotating between 40 to 45 degrees celcius in Gujarat we heard the noise of someone cutting a tree in one of the outskirts of the palace but beyond the boundary wall though it was boiling hot and the heat was unbearable in the afternoon my father immediately called for the sepoy on duty at the palace gate and the two of them started marching towards that direction of the noise bearing the burning heat of the sun.   , Just out of curiosity I asked my father if I could join them on this adventurous trip? Of course, he said provided you can bear the extreme heat, crossing the walled compound we reached one of the corners of the palace compound next reaching the tennis court as it was called consisting of a couple of huge Neem trees, on one of which a waghri was merrily perched cutting a huge branch without realizing or sensing our arrival.

On standing underneath the sepoy accompanying us drew the attention of this carefree waghri and asked him to climb down, on noticing us standing right beneath him and recognizing my father he panicked and as soon as he climbed down he fell at my father's feet asking for forgiveness. My father asked him to getup and leave the premises immediately if not he will be handed over to the police for stealing. Thanking my father for forgiving him he picked up his Axe and sprinted for his life soon out of sight.

After a couple of days again in the midst of a summer night the same sound was heard almost from the same direction, this time too I accompanied the investigation team, out of sheer curiosity, hence we followed the same exercise of reaching the place of its origin and to my great surprise I found the same person axing another Neem tree close to the one we had caught him on and let him go. This time he had noticed us coming towards him as we had used long dry cell torches to find our way in the midst of the night which he may have noticed approaching him but before he could fully alight and dash out of the compound we had caught hold of him once again, he started pleading for forgiveness and turning to my father he said sahib, "I have small children to feed and though I am a daily wager last couple of days in spite of my best efforts I am unable to get any work, hence, I was forced to steal to feed my hungry children by cutting this tree which could be sold for a few rupees to buy food for my family."

Though initially annoyed on seeing the same waghri my father spoke to him very politely after hearing his pathetic story. "OKAY said my father, but why do you steal from Nawab Sahibs compound if you need money to feed your children come to my office and I will give you some work, but please don't steal, and urged him to look for a job tomorrow again and probably if you still you are unable to find one come down to my office and I may provide you with some temporary work on daily wages but for God's sake don't do something wrong."

Once again he touched my father's feet and left the compound coming down to the palace office on and off for odd jobs which Dad used to give him whenever the occasion arouse.

On the walk back from the tennis court compound I remember having asked my Dad why was he so polite to the waghri inspite of his being warned once not to enter the compound and cut the trees?

I also remember well what he had replied "Abbas he must have really been in need of money to feed his hungry children if not he won't have done it the second time in such a situation it was necessary to make him understand politely not to adopt a permanent wrong path but to make an extra effort to earn his livelihood honestly besides he is also a human being and the love of his children and the pangs of their hunger may have driven him to take a risk again to commit a wrong. My son always be God fearing and understand the intention of the other it will take you a long way".

Quite true some 30 years later when my father passed off at AHMEDABAD as per his wishes he was buried at Cambay/Khambhat on the third day after the burial which is customarily known as the "ziyarat" day a number of persons had called at our house at Khambhat to offer their condolences even some whom I was not well acquainted with, however I recognized the wood cutter waghri though seeing him after over 30 years, he had become old and haggered but his voice had not changed much, he approached both my brother and my self and wept at first then showered all the praise one can think of on the life of the departed soul but his parting lines cannot be forgotten. "In the present times it may not be possible to get such a benevolent man like your father,... Saheb".

This complement was enough to make me realise the love, affection and respect my father had cultivated by being just kind and compassionate to the poor and the needy at the same time full filling his duties as a humble caretaker of all that belonged to the Nawab saheb Jaffer Ali Khan Najmessani and the entire royal family who I am sure will unhesitating bare testimony to my claim about my late father.

Its always been my good fortune that whenever we meet the Royal family of Khambhat each member never stops remembering him and complementing him endlessly.

Dedicated to my late Father who has been a role model to me in many principles I pursued in both my personal and professional life.

WHEN FEAR STRIKES !

Having spent my childhood in the premises of a huge palace along with my brother and parents which was generally vacant as Nawab Saheb had shifted to Bombay the fear of darkness and imaginative Ghost non existed in us, (In fact I feel my brother is more fearless than my self) hence in my school and college days hearing morbid Ghost tales of horror never instilled the sense of fear in me. This quality of not believing in ghosts and spirits was known to my friend Naushad who in one of the ghost stories session of his college clique braged about it in his elite circle on hearing about the streak of fearless- ness in me,and Naushad bragging about it, a common friend from this circle who also lived at Bandra wanted to prove his bravery to this (Naushad) circle or gang in college, challenged him and said that if your friend Abbas is so fearless I would not mind having a bet with him to prove who's more valiant/brave. When Naushad narrated this challenge, Right I replied anytime lets have a bet and see who's more 'bahadur' so a sum of 100/-Rupees was decided as the winners purse which in those days meant a reasonably good amount of dough for a lavish treat.

Now pondering over how to prove our valour it was decided that at 12 midnight both the aspirants should enter a graveyard cross it alone and collect a souvenir from inside the cemetery to be presented as proof of having crossed it hence after a lot of searching by common friends it was finalized that I with Naushad and he with his friend would meet outside St.Andrew's church at Hill Road Bandra at 12 in the night cross the cemetery and collect the proof and return unshattered/unaffected.

I readily agreed to this proposal and added that there is a tank at far end corner of this church cum cemetery in which the discarded skeletons and bones are dumped, hence the challenger should open this tank collect a piece of skeleton bone from it and get it back as proof to those standing outside, on adding this supplementary requirement I had noticed a deep sense of fear which had already crept in the eyes of my competitors.

As for myself I could not have asked for a better exercise to prove myself as during my schooling days the standard 3rd and 4th of my school St. Andrew's high school due to shortage of classroom were held in the church compound and premises and thus I was familiar with its surroundings during these two years, I had personally seen number of funerals and burial at this church, infact I remember seeing a number of old graves being dug up with remains of skeletons and bones which used to be collected and thrown in this far off corner tank at the far end of the church.

It was finally 12 midnight for the decider and so Naushad and myself were standing outside the St.Andrew's church gate only to find my brave friends turnup 12:15 looking quite disturbed, right from the beginning, having exchanged cordialities Naushad tossed a coin to decide who would enter the graveyard first, he won the toss and I was certain that he would ask me to get in first.

Being mentally prepared for this adventure, I immediately entered the church compound and crossed it briskly in the direction of the tank reached it but did not open its lid fearing some ghosts would come out instead of a human bone that I was required to collect ? I picked up a piece of broken white marble kept on top of the tank's lid ! The night was quite and there was darkness around and hence I felt quite scared too..... so I closed my eyes and ran back towards the huge entrance gate where my friends were waiting on the other side. The whole exercise may have lasted about 6 to 8 minutes and at last on reaching the gate and the bright street lights I intentionally dropped the piece of marble at the feet of the group when the big marble piece splintered into many white pieces and I just uttered "O.K. now its your turn pal".

On seeing the broken marble pieces at their feet, white in colour thought perhaps to be piece of bones of a skeleton, they panicked turning around and without uttering a word both bolted homeward with both running as if a real Ghost was behind them.

Naushad too stood dazed for a while and we both looked at each other and laughed to our hearts content. I then dusted my hands and the two of us walked back home renewing our commitment to meet at the Perry road bus stop at 8 in the morning.

On reaching college next day ,we kept a strict vigil for the brave man to appear but the whole day neither he or his good friend were to be seen so we asked this group as to what had happened to the tough Macho guy? just when one of the girl from his group informed us that when she rang up his residence sometime back the brave man's mother informed her that he and his friends after returning late in the night were shivering and developed high fever, God knows what happened added the mother but they had a lot of fear written all over them and perhaps were too shocked to say anything. This morning I had to take them to the Doctor who could actually not dicognised their illness"

On hearing this the whole group had a hearty laugh and someone remarked that if they don't get well soon Naushad you and your friend may soon be charged under some pinal section of code for frightening the hell out of them now this remark really sounded alarming at the same time amusing so I mumbled to Naushad "Bawa, discretion is always better part of valour, chal pher miltehai" and walked off from his group.

LOOKING FOR TROUBLE OR A TRIPLE ?

Naushad belongs to the Ginwalla family who have horse racing to their blood and being a good friend this vice had rubbed out on me, to some extent hence during the racing season at the Bombay Turf club at Manalaxmi we were regular visitors to the course practically every Sunday during the season.

The COLE book in those days was so sacred to us then any other holly book sent from the heavens …as we regiously bought it every Friday while returning from college… thoroughly studied it from the moment we entered he suburban train and back home from Marine lines to Bandra slept with it for the next two days until we reached the Turf club and till all the events got over for the day.

As a rule we generally used to lose more than we ever gained but the charm and excitement of watching the horses run and loseing our pocket money had almost become and addiction.

As maybe known to regulars the entry to the racecourse is divided into three categories.

a.)   The members enclosure

b.)   The first enclosure

c.)   The second enclosure

Coming from a fairly decent background we could afford the first enclosure as the second enclosure consisted more of Riffraff's from which we had the sixth sense to keep away. However, we had developed a reasonably good friendship with one Ahmed Cha-cha of the second enclosure (who was almost a regular like us and on account of his experience and knowledge on which horse to bet, this chacha was generally dressed in a white kurta Pajama with a large checkered kerchief hanging on his shoulder he was a paan addict thus a regular stream of red paan salaiva regularly seeped down on both sides of his lower lip, being middle aged he would walk very leisurely towards the bookie RING where we often used to meet him and crosscheck our assessment of the horses.

Chacha as informed earlier was very found of betting in the ring where private bookies offer higher stakes as compared to the official Turf club tote. The entry to the ring is open to patrons of all enclosure and is situated in the middle of the three stands erected for viewing the events.

Now one fine Sunday it so happened that we were not sure, about a horse to be played in a particular race and frantically wanted chacha's expert advice and opinion as to which horse to put our money on so were desperately trying to locate him just then we saw him moving in his usual leisurely style towards the ring at the same time a suited gentleman from the members stand from the opposite gangway was also advancing towards the ring with his attention focused on the Cole book and collieded head on with our race course chacha on regaining his posture the gentleman at first looked at the chacha, From top to toe who seemed quite amused at this emaculate man bumping into him and further still not accepting his fault... by this time we too had reached the site of collusion the next moment the gentleman without acknowledging his fault dusted his coat moved a little back and shouted at Ahmed chacha quite loudly "looking for trouble"? The amused chacha did not know much of English and misunderstanding the statement of the   gentleman said

"MIYA EK GODA NAHEE LEGTA TRIPLE KE KYA BHAT KARTHE HO "!

(The English translation = Gentle man , ' Unable to get a single winning Horse, how can you ask for a triple?)

Ha ha ha , Now the poor gentleman did not know what to do and left the scene in a huff as we started laughing at the answer given by Ahmed chacha. This unique Chacha's answer line has since become one of our favorite line whenever we want to express our anguish in many a hopeless situation!

(A VISIT) TO HELL AND BACK

Besides Naushad I had only a few very good friends in college, though my circle of acquaintances was quite large it was only a few whom I could call my "Jigari Dost" Mario being one of them.

Now Mario(Rao) had joined the Taj hotel at Bombay as a front office receptionist as his father had passed off while he was in college with us and was the only brother to four sisters hence responsibility of looing after the family had fallen on him earlier than expected, which he tried to full fill quite religiously.

Since Mario was at the Taj a place known for its celebrity patronage and expose to the elite I never missed an opportunity to visit him whenever the opportunity arose, during one of my visits I found Mario involved in conversation with an unfamiliar girl as most of the girls at the reception desk were known to me as I kept visiting him at least once a week.

On reaching them Mario said hello to me and promptly introduced me to this girl who happened to be a Bengali quite pleasant and attractive to look at, on exchanging pleasantries she told me that she worked in one of the boutiquesof the Taj shopping Arcade and asked me to drop-in sometime.

Meeting Naushad that evening I told him about the Bengali girl who was quite fascinating and added that he must see her as she was very charming. After a couple of days we went shopping to Colaba from college and after having bought a pair of shoes we decided to meet Mario at Taj which was quite close by, on reaching Taj we were informed at the reception that Mario was not on duty that day so we almost decided to go back before which Naushad thought of some window shopping at the Taj Arcade before going home just then I remembered why not to drop in at the Bengali girls boutique since we had come all the way to the Taj, so we casually found her shop and dropped in only to be delighted by her welcome she recognized me at once and was all smiles on seeing us I introduced her to Naushad and as there were no customers at that time we saw some shirts at the boutique and chatted about Sunday issues for quite sometime.

When it was time for us to leave I really don't know why ? just before leaving I asked her "what time do you wind up " she said 7 7:30 p.m., so what do you do in the evening "nothing in particular " she answered then my madness drew me to ask her what she is doing to night? nothing she answered instead questioned me what are you doing to night ? Naushad and myself were quite amazed at her boldness and kept looking at each other just then I casually replied going to hell, she said that's one Disco I have not seen... so what ! Naushad butted in Abbas will take you there "when she said jokingly 'tonight itself"   ' if you permit me' I retorted and she almost shocked us when she added "provided we go out in a four-some" Naushad froze for a while at her super boldness looked at me again and said 'Bawa then lets go out tonight'…. first I will callup Shireen and then fix up pops car, alright anything for you Miya. This was around 4 p.m. and having sealed the date we split fixing to pick her up between 8 8"30 from her place somewhere in Byculla soon we were out of her shop and the Taj and Naushad could not wait to accept she was faster than he thought and winked and added 'Miya your life's made this evening'…. to which I answered intuitively "let us not count the chickens before the eggs are hatched!"

Right those were not mobile phone days so we hurriedly called Shireen from an outside booth. Now Shireen was a good friend of Naushad he could always rely on her, she worked as a receptionist at a leading Doctors clinic at camps comer and left for home around 8 p.m., at first Shireen was reluctant to go out that night at such a short notice but finally agreed when Naushad told her the whole story she asked Nash to pass on the phone to me and said ' anything for a friend.'

Naushad had a tough time convincing his pop to let us have the car for the night and somehow we managed to put the whole act together picking up Shireen from her Pedder road residence at 8:30 reaching the Bengali baby's after 9 putting her also in the car and heading for the discotheque Hell at Worli seaface on the way we stopped for some up chat-puri and Panipuri bought our cigarettes and were found buying the entrance tickets of Hell at 10:30 that night.

on entering the pshycodalic lite disco we found the dance floor just warming up the dance numbers too were not so hectic so after jumping around for about half and hour on the floor we felt the atmosphere was not much to our liking hence we decided to either sit over a bottle of coke or take a stroll or a drive and get back when the scene became more jubilant we thus cooked up a story of having lost a wallet at the entrance to allow us to go look for it and get back later on the same tickets…….

Having managed that with great difficulty we got out of the disco and went for a drive to chowpatty and further still to the gateway of India since the Bengali baby worked at the Taj she did not want to get out of the car when we suggested the idea of having a stroll and a smoke down there to kill sometime and then get back.   Having lite our cigarettes Naushad just jokingly remarked that our cigarettes were loaded with Hash hearing this she taught it to be true and seriously asked for a puff as she had never tried it and wanted to taste it for the first time I was a little stumped to hear that but I got into the back seat where she was sitting and jokingly gave her my cigarette to have a puff of the presumed hash, Shireen then got into the front seat of the Fiat car with Naushad and we happily drove off from the gateway, Shireen also taught there was some haas in the cigarette and so she too wanted to take it and had a puff from Naushad fag as we were merrily cruseing along back to Worli Sea face when my date asked me for a second puff I gave her my fag once again and this time she had 2 or 3 big drags from the cigarette and started coughing, then yelling and finally crying, screaming aloud 'I hate him, I hate him ' which grew louder and louder and drew the attention of the passersby.

Naushad on seeing this unexpected behavior of this girl reacted quite stunned and asked me and Shireen to pull up the glasses of the windows least she draws the attention from outside and creates a scene of the road but she did not stop at that and went hysterical and beserk so we just kept on driving and driving….. so that she may calm down and get back to normal… she would slow down a little after a peak but would burst out crying the moment we thought of stoping some where to pack her off in a cab along with Shireen to her house at Byculla, however she would just not stop or clam down and kept on repeating the sentence a number of time 'I hate him, I hate him' and splutter the choiest of abuses and become hysterical once again creating a tense atmosphere in the car.

In the midst of this commotion she admitted to being madly in love with some one who worked at the Taj hotel and that she had a tiff with him just yesterday and just to teach him a lesson (she thought) she had come out with us. Never the less she won't stop crying and the 3 of us were quite panicked fearing it to be misconstrued as a case of abduction or something which the police could cook up as she was less than 18 years of age.

Driving countless miles atlast the fuel needle started moving towards the empty side it was nearing 4 in the morning pampering this babe all over Bombay from Gateway to Bandra circle and back a couple of times when at last Naushad stopped the car abruptly at a lonely place and asked Shireen to exchange places with me then told her in Gujarati to given her 2 to 3 tight slaps Shireen gave her a couple of hard slaps which perhaps brought her back to her senses then gave her a piece of her mind on her atrocious behavior, Alas she stoped crying and came back to reality and started apologizing. We asked her to be only quite which will help us solve the mess she had created we first spotted a day night petrol pump filled up some fuel and quickly wanted to drop her and Shireen at Pedder road and then reached Byculla at 5:30 in the morning my parting line whilst dropping her back was a sarcastic "thank you very much for everything!"

On the way back Naushad hailed the choicest of abuses on me and asked me to swear never to go out with girls we didn't know. Thank god he added it was a close shave……. for this girl had made all plans for us to land up in the clinkers!

The next day I rang up Mario at the Taj and narrated the whole horrible episode, probably he may have pulled her up for her stupid behavior too ! when I met him next after a few days this time at his residence, Mario said the Bengali babe has sent you her apologies and says you are a very sweet guy she ready toforget the whole episode and become good friends.

I laughed aloud folded my hands and asked Mario to convey my humble regrets with the same gusto "wasn't one night enough for us to go to hell and were just lucky enough to get back!"

CHAR DIN KI CHANDNI

As detailed in a previous episode the itch of betting on horses at the Turf club' of Bombay and Pune had really got the better of us and it was nothing new for us to walk back home many a time from Bandra station after returning from Mahalaxmi course with the hope to win in the last race... betting even our last penny and go home rich perhaps. Our student railway pass was a blessing in disguise as we could conveniently use it from Mahalaxmi in Bandra though it was allotted to us for travel from Bandra to Marinelines as students of St.Xaviers College if not would have found us walking back home from Mahalaxmi to perry road Bandra probably?

However the law of averages always has its run and one fine racing day it so happened that Naushad and myself agreed on the winner of certain races identically and to our great surprise it happened to be played in the triple pot, which means all your win in the first race is transferred to the second and the second to the third hence eventually if you call the right horses in all three one stands to take home a big amount that night so this time we took a chance and played some combination for a Triple at the Turf club tote.

As luck would have it one of the combinations clocked on a ticket of some 10 to 12/- odds and so we managed to collect somewhere close to 20000/- bucks!

big money by any standards in the 70's. Having cracked this amount we just could not believe our luck and went mad with joy and excitement. Naushad insisted we go back home in a cab to compensate the many walks from Bandra railway station to home , OK Bawa I said on our way back we stopped at a store bought ourselves a couple of foreign cigarette packets Dunhill/Rothmans if I recall correctly and Cadbury chocolates by the time we reached home it was late evening and a Bandra Gymkhana ball was scheduled for that nite with entry tickets of some 100 to 150/- per person we would easily afford that tonite and decided to really live it up by having a great party that night at the Gymkhana lawns.

Getting this opportunity we went all suited booted and colonged blew up some more money on food and Frolick danced till early morning with some known girls from our perry road area who were pleasantly surprised to find us too there.

Next morning when we met at the 221 junction bus stop we calculated our expenses and arrived at a Balance of 18000/- net rest all blown up the night before. Money never mattered between the solid friendship bond which existed between Naushad and myself infact he was generally the cashier between the two of us as he liked to carry money with or on him which was perfectly okay by me.

Now Naushad used to bet at the Matka occasionally with which I was not too familiar hence on his suggestion to increase our kitty sufficiently enough to buy a second hand car and show off in it was quite inviting and worth dreaming of? The odds in Matka are 1 is to 9 for predicting the single card right and 1:81 for predicting a double. Now Naushad said we will only put 4000/- on stake and try our luck not the whole amount being so good buddies I had no cause to dispute his decision and disturb our combined dream of buying a second hand sports model convertible and driving in it along the carter road beach in a silk shirt with a scarf in the neck and the hair flying in the evening sunset breeze etc…H ha So we bet the amount on the first day which turned out to be luckless, on the second day Naushad thought he count go wrong but that too went fuss so on he third day we were left with just 4000/- as we were blowing up the money at the same time entertaining our friends and buying clothes, perfumes and accessories.

This time Naushad was quite certain that it would click and that we would get back rich like last Sunday so we played the whole amount on a double but everyday is not Sunday and the inevitable happened our aakhridao was also lost.I remember it was a 95, the first nine opened in the first round but the second round let us down again at 12'Oclock in the dead of the night. After nothing the results at 12 that night we went numb for while but the next moment we looked at each other and had a hearty laugh dusted our hands and went back home as usual.

On the forth day we were once again standing at the Perry road bus stop junction waiting for the BEST bus route no. 221 to take us to the railway station consoling each other for losing all the money by recalling the hectic time we had from the moment of wining it to time of losing it all. These four days were indeed moment one would rarely forget in life.Char din ke chandni ?

THE MURDER OF THE OLD ARM CHAIR

I used to stay at perry road in Bandra at the Nawab Saheb's bunglow opposite across the road was a bunglow belonging to a parsee family consisting memebrs of three generation i.e. The grandpa his son and wife and two daughters and an attended a surti servant.

The family was undoubtedly very decent except that Grandpa was very boisterous sitting out in the varandha every morning and evening on an easy arm chair passing unending comments and remarks on matters not concerning him in fact at times we would fall into the habit of giving a running commentary on events to even passers by.

Naushad stayed down the road and not bang opposite this Grandpa'sbunglow, never the less whenever he happened to pass this place and get noticed by Grandpa sitting outside on his easy chair the oldman never let go the opportunity of passing a remark on him perhaps since Naushad too was a parsee or of the same age as his grand daughters, in whom Naushad he as a matter of fact was not the least interested.

This habit of Grandpa was so irritating to Naushad that at time he would turn back and go home if he saw from a far the old man sitting on his chair in the varandha, many a time I used to tell Naushad not to pay attention to what he says and the poor old man does not have anything interesting to do but to pass his time, so has fallen into the habit of making weird comments which we should overlook or ignore.

Generally after dinner Naushad and myself used to go out for a walk at the carter road beach sit on the boundary wall separating the sea beach from the road and analyse the days events till well past midnight before returning home. It so happened on night that Naushad wanted to collect some notes from me so he accompanied me to my house just them he noticed the old man's chair lying in his varandha. An evil glimmer lite his eyes and he told me in a whisper the chairs lying today without the cribbing oldman on it, so what Bawa how many times have I told you just to ignore that side. No, No, today I am going to teach him a lesson I will get this chair and hide it or throw It into the sea atleast he will not be seen outside for quite some time.

I kept murmuring No, No but before I knew anything in a flash Naushad opened the gate of the bunglow entered the house picked up the chair and ran out, I was stranded at the gate and on seeing him running with the chair closed the gate and ran behind him he crossed the road and ran towards my house I didn't know what to do and before I could say some thing he had entered our compound and was running towards my room. Luckily no one saw us perform the theft on reaching my room we took some breath I yelled at Naushad for this madness but he kept on saying that he wanted to teach the old man a lesson and so he just did it.

Anyway now what's to be done? Tomorrow the old man's going to hit the roof when he finds his chair missing and it is going to be headline news of perry road area. So what's to be done we than started thinking ? at first we thought we could break it and throw it an all direction, but breaking it was not going to be easy so Naushad asked me to get some kerosene from the kitchen having done that we slowly carried it to the terrace poured the kerosene on it and torched it. It started burning for a while and ultimately only the remaining few pieces of wood where left unburnt which we picked and threw it in all different directions from the terrace with all our might, we mopped up the terrace floor and washed it with a bucket of water to get rid of any traces of the stolen murdered and burnt to death chair!

Having completed this operation we sat contented in my room shared a fag and saw off Naushad to the gate asking him to meet as usual 8:30 am at the bus stop which was our daily routine and so all seems normal and none gets the slightest hint of our secret operation.

We met as usual at the bus stop infact Naushad was there before me curious to know the after effects from across the road of the exertion, when I reached him I told him I heard a lot of hauling and granting from across the road and from the house but I didn't see your friend Grandpa atleast I just heard their comments. Thank God he taught, but just ten later we saw their servant a dark man with a south Gujarati accent approach us we froze for a while and taught the cat is out of the bag perhaps, but he came close and whispered into Naushad's ears that the old man's chair is stolen last night and that we all should become very careful as robbers and thieves have struck this street for the first time and may followup with acts of greater robberies, however, it was good that Dadaji's chair was stolen for it was full of bed bugs and the family feels quite relieved as it was a good riddens to bad (bug) rubbish, just then the 221 bus arrived and we were only too happy to get into it and leave for Bandra railway station on the way to the college we felt happy and releaved that the whole parsee family will infact feel happy at the loss of the chair except the Grumpy old Grandpa and may just stop sitting outside in the varandha passing his silly remarks.

However, on returning back from college that evening and feeling not the least guilty for the murder of the chair and its clueless disposal we were in for an anticlimax when we saw the cherpy old man found sitting on a brand New arm chair presented by his son and instead of the usual 5 pm he had ventured out into the varandha of his bunglow at 4 that evening calling all passers by and telling them how his old beloved arm chair was stolen last night and that one should become very vigilant to nab the culprits before they venture in to some thing bigger.

Naushad almost tripped when Grandpa saw him and called "Dikra" i.e. son please come here. I want to caution you, oh no not again mumbled Naushad probably. I will have to totally stop coming to your house to avoid these sermons as I can never think of stealing his chair once again and going through the process of disposing it off once again!!

THAT SOLID PUNCH

After completing graduation and my diploma in marketing management I was very keen to go and work outside the country and earn some good amount of money return back after a couple of years and take up some other job or start a business which could help my family and myself leading a comfortable life in the future but since my Dad was against the idea of my leaving the country I decided to settle down in Ahmedabad got married to the daughter of my mother's childhood friend and became a father much earlier to my childhood buddies being initially blessed with a baby girl.

Naushad was unable to attend my marriage and it was only after a year and half after my daughter birth that he decided to come down to Ahmedabad to pay a visit at my humble dwelling.

Naushad's parents incidentally belonged to Ahmedabad and his maternal Grand father's bungalow known as the colonel Nanavatis bunglow adjacent to GPO at Ahmedabad was lying vacant, hence when he came down on this visit he stayed at this place inspite of his cousin and or insistence inviting him to stay with us, I presume it was mainly because he had come down with another cousin from Bombay and did not wish to burden us for arranging facilities of boarding for the two.

However, during his flying visit to Ahmedabad on the second evening we decided to have dinner outside at a famous Goanese restaurant near St. Xaviers school Mirzapur, after dinner we took a stroll on Nehru Bridge and while returning Naushad resorted to some college days pranks whilst walking back from the Nehru bridge to the bunglow at GPO of making fun of an old wired looking pedestrian just opposite Rupali Cinema. This man was quite agitated and started shouting at Naushad and some tough roughen belonging to this area and known to the old man who happened to pass by caught hold of Naushad by the collar and after a brief argument slapped him real hard and won't leave him off, I tried real hard by shouting louder than him to leave Naushad but he won't just let him go, infact the one who had held him taunted me and told me that he just wouldn't leave Naushad and wanted to know what I would do to release him? This argument really aggrivated me to lose my shirt, hence I gathered all my strength and gave him such a solid blow on his face that he just collapsed, so Naushad was let off and we ran for our lives, followed by the crowd which had gathered around us and probably people known to the roughen on seeing him collapse ran after me caught up with me around the Mosque and just let me have it with kicks and blows it was a free for all kind of a show luckily having learnt to box in school and college I buried my face in between my arms and croached downwards till they could kick me no more left me and walked away as they saw a policeman approaching.

The policeman asked me what happened I told him the whole story he told me that they were all seasoned goondas of this area and that I was lucky not to be knifed he told me to go and look for my friends, least they may be caught and hamered as well.

I was certain they coun't have been caught as they both bolted like wild horses. Though battered I managed to find my way back to the Nanavati bungalow where both my friends had put off the lights at the entrance and were hiding in the dark on hearing my voice they hesitatingly opened the door and informed me in umpteen burst of laughter that they had witnessed the battering I got from a lane far off but were hesitant and afraid to come and retrieve me from the slaughter, however they were all praise for the massive blow I landed on the roughen which just knocked him off instantly even the noise it emitted was solid.

Any way this episode was soon forgotten none the lesson one of my visits to Bombay long after Naushad got married and had kids his son asked me to narrate this episode as he wanted to hear or know it from the horses mouth. I told him of the solid punch which had knocked the Rupali roughen and I also told him why I done so, that was to retrieve your pop from the goonda, in conclusion he turned around and said but pop never told me about the solid slap which he got , I then had my last laugh and told his son Nash one should always hear the unedited version, Naushad was out on a flight that day so I left his house with the parting line, "son when your pop comes back please confirm to me on phone if he still remembers that slap? Which propelled me to deliver 'THAT solid punch!!

MY RSS CONNECTION

It was in the year late 1979 that I was selected as a sales officer of Spencer and Co. Ltd to look after and sales of consumer durable products of the Co. in Gujarat. This was perhaps my first regular job in a well established all India Co. besides obtaining this position it was also quite a competitive process/exercise at the early stage of my working career.

Products such as refrigerators, air conditioners, air coolers vacuum cleaners were sold and serviced by us through a dealer network spread all over Gujarat.

The company had its Branch office at Ahmedabad which consisted of a staff of some 20 persons which worked under the Zonal office at Bombay. Shri B. Vishvanathan the Zonal manager was the highest authority of the company in the west and generally visited Ahmedabad every second month to review the affairs/status of the company's Gujarat business and its progress.

Shri Philips Serao was the Branch manager at Gujarat and Mr. Shridharan was the Accountant. One fine morning in the second month after joining. I heard of Mr. Vishvanathan visit to Ahmedabad, the Zonal manager used to come down by Air putup at the affluent Cama Hotel and an A/C Taxi was kept in waiting right from the time of his arrival to departure, from the little I gathered about him it was evident that he was a head task master in the office and a leading worker of the RSS in his personal capacity, where he used to drop in whenever the opportunity arouse, hence, I tickled my sixth sense to find out the venue of the RSS H.O. at Ahmedabad and since one of my uncle's stayed close-by, took the trouble of ascertaining its venue personally. The day Vishvanathan Saheb arrived at Ahmedabad the Company office was at its best behavior, however during this visit sales were sluggish and the outstandings had reached some enormous proportions which eneraged the Zonal manager to a great extent and so he called the Accountant in the B.M.'s cabin and gave them both a good piece of his mind being comparatively new to the company I was spared the ordeal and was sitting outside when Shri Vishvanathan fretting and fumling walked out of the cabin saw me sitting quite petrified at the shouting inside and gestured to me to come a long, on joining him he asked me if I knew the location of the RSS? Pat came my answer "yes sir" then call the cab and lets go there "right, sir" very soon we were at the entrance of the RSS office and so Vishvanathan Saheb asked me to go inside and inform the head Pramukh that Shri B. Vishvanathan of Madras has come,... I did exactly as told, hence on learning about this visit the whole atmosphere in the RSS became electrifying as Vishvanathanji was a very tall leader of the Sangh and they wanted to accord him a befitting welcome so they requested me to hold him in the car for some 10 minutes before I could get him down to the entrance once again, I did exactly as told and when we actually entered a big royal welcome was awaiting us followed by Tea/snacks at the Ahmedabad RSS Branch.......

Before leaving Vishvanathan assured the Ahmedabad RSS head that I i.e. A.G. Mehdi would be visiting the Shakha at least twice a month and if they needed anything it could be conveyed to me quite frankly, thus began my association with the RSS, which I visited quite religiously every forthnight and sent a personal line to the Zonal Manager that all was well… fortunately for me during that period at least.

Soon my 6 months probation was coming to an end, and so my file was sent to Ahmedabad for the B.M's remarks which was good as sales had started improving and outstanding had droped down drastically then came the Zonal manager turn at Bomay and the file was put up for his opinion and signature. The moment he read my full name Abbas Ghulam Mehdi, Mr Vishvanathan hastened to call the HR man in the presence of his P.A. Mrs. Kripalani (who told me the story later).

As soon as the HR person arrived Vishvanathanji immediately asked him "Did you know Mehdi is a muslim ?" Yes, sir" he answered, "who has selected him"? he added "you took the final interview sir" was the answer "Oh, yes, I forgot, Okay confirm him immediately with an appropriate increment, he has really shown very good results at Ahmedabad which should be appreciated".

Within the next 2 days I received my confirmation with an increment letter delivered through the Branch Manager who could not believe the appreciation from the Zonal HQ and remarked what magic I had used to deserve this blue eyed treatment?

However, after another fortnight I once again heard of the Zonal Manager's visit and this time the Branch Manager asked me to accompany him to the Airport to receive him, on having received him and dropping him at the Cama hotel Shri Vishvanathan asked me to come up to his room after about 10 minutes. Philips Serao my BM and boss was quite surprised at this invitation and proceeded to our office at Relief road quietly with a stoic look on his face.

Having spent those 10 minutes wandering what's in store for me I finally reached his room rang the bell and was asked to make myself comfortable and call for pot tea from the room service department as he was having a wash to fresh up for the office visit.

On joining me he questioned me on the status of sales and payments of the Gujarat dealers then talked in general about news of the day, however , when tea was serviced (by the waiter) and we were in the midst of it he very casually remarked "Mehdi" you never told me you were a muslim? perhaps, I was anticipating this and my immediate answer was "you never asked me, sir" he laughed quite heartily at my instant witty reply and added I am sorry, I was unaware when I entrusted you with the task of visiting the RSS office at Ahmedabad. "no, no sir I did not mind it in the least, infact I kept on doing it as a duty and even built up a good report with the people there" was my answer "Okay now I think you should stop this assignment!" "Right, sir".

This gentleman always appreciated me and within 2 years I was promoted as a Branch Manager of spencer's Pune.

Now that's my sweet experience of the connections I had with the RSS and the wonderful, Godfather I found in Shri Vishvanathan Saheb of Spencer and Co. Ltd. Madras, the tall leader from the RSS!

A SACRED BOND

Having tied the knot in July 1975 I started working as a sales executive with a distributor of Usha pistons for the state of Gujarat this was my first full time job and the much awaited exposure of practical marketing which was quite different to the theoretical knowledge I had acquired in pursuing a diploma in Advertising and Marketing from Bombay. After marriage since we opted to stay independently of our parents in Ahmedabad and since my monthly salary was only Rs 600/- a month we had to budget our income towards expenses such as house rent, kitchen expenses, etc. making it compulsory for us to spend our income prudently, at times the last week before salary was a tough period to pull throw comfortably. To make ends meet and earn some additional income, I was always open to an opportunity to travel on tours and earn some extra income from the company, being in such a situation it was advisible to practice family planning as we really could not afford the expense of having a baby, however after a year income increased from a hike in the salary and more income from out station tours, so we thought of having a baby and though my wife conceived in January 1977 she told me about it in the month of March the exact date I don't remember but perhaps one of happiest days of my life, I was on sky seven having learnt of becoming a father.

Soon after, we consulted one of the best orthopedic doctors of Ahmedabad and followed it up with all precautions required to be taken by a lady on the family way. I would try to bring home the best of food and fruits advised by the doctor and accompany my wife to the clinic on all her checkups, during these days my younger brother got married to my wife's younger sister and we took all the care to be a part of the marriage ensuring Nishat was not the least put to any kind of strain in her pregnancy.

A few days before the due date we shifted to my inlaws residence at kinarewala building Gaikewad Haveli (Ahmedabad) registering Nishat's name even at the Government maternity home next door just in case of an emergency.

The expected happened and my wife developed some pain in the dead of the night at 2 am and when my inlaws took her to the maternity home the maid after having checked her adviced my mother-in-law to admit her immediately as she was going through her labour pains and would deliver the baby any moment, my daughter was born at around 3:30 am in the morning and though I was at the hospital I got to see them at around 5 in the morning of October the 7th 1977 on being allowed inside the room I first went to my wife as I was usually concerned about her health she was quite well and smiling and then she pointed to our baby who was fast asleep all wraped in a cot next to her bed the first time I saw Shahzi my daughter she looked so clam and beautiful, from that moment a sacred bond between a father and a daughter took birth also which continues till today, on being discharged from the government maternity home all I had to pay was 125/- even today we keep on wondering how reasonable were those times and period for just a single visit to a general practitioner today cost much more!

Shahzi my daughter has become a big girl today and has shifted to London with her husband (our son-n-law) Hassan infact the roles are quite reversed today for she keeps on inquiring and caring for us as we had done when she was a little baby and we would do all we could to give her the best. Perhaps life is a cycle preserved of course by a sacred bond of Love, love between parents and their children and vice-versa over endless period of time.

A PRAYER FULLFILLED

After joining spencer and Co. as a sales executive at Ahmedabad to market consumer durables such A/c, fridge, vaccum cleaners, water coolers, etc. consumer products such as vijay Ghee and cheese and spencer pharmaceuticals I was transferred to Pune as a Branch manager of newly opened Branch of the company to control the central and south Maharashtra region, by my RSS God father Shri Vishvanathan Saheb.

This was in the year 1980 after finding a house in the Pune camp area on rent with great difficulty I shifted my family there too admitted my daughter in the school and started controlling the area seriously marketing all its different categories of products. This exercise gave me an exposure of independently handling the sales service and administration of a Branch. I was also exposed to the Central and southern part of Maharashtra that consists of the rich sugar cane belt towns such as Sanghli, Satara, Kolhapur, Sholapur, Aurangabad etc, which were frequently visited by me for marketing assignments and the branch operations.

The climate of Pune was very pleasant and the people too were very friendly infact Pune was one of the best postings I have ever received in my working career.

Though my salary had increased as a Branch Manager. The rent cost of acquiring an independent house in the Pune camp area and the standard of livin was higher to that of Ahmedabad was streaching my purse hence, I had to always work harder and travel more to earn that extra buck which now became more of a necessity for keeping my family reasonably comfortable.

As luck would have it my wife conceived again at Pune and we started consulting an orthopedic lady doctor Miss Dalla at the Jehangir Nursing home at Pune, Doctor Dalla was very strict as regards to the food and tonic she would prescribe to my wife and wanted Nishat to meet all Targets of tonics and exercises given to her during the fornightly checkups.

The due date as given by Dr.Dalla was middle of February hence as we were staying alone I had requested my inlaws to come down to Pune by the 1st week of February to help us in this period and my mother in law along with my Brother in law had even made their railway reservations accordingly....to come down to Pune and help us .... 26th January Republic Day was a holiday and we at home spent it quite happily together watching DD programs on the T.V. which was supposed to be a luxury in those days as very few houses in the society possessed one and whenever there was an evening movie on a Sunday on the Door Darshan all the next door neighbours would fill my living room in which the T.V. set was kept! 27th

I attended office at Pune and was planning to go out on tour from 28th January. for a couple of days.

It was around 11:30 that night Nishat started getting some pain since it was not subsiding till 12 midnight we called the neighbours wife who advised us to rush to the maternity home, since the society where we were staying was more on the outskirts of Pune even a. 3 wheeler or any other means of public transport was Not available, hence I had no choice but ask my wife to pillon ride on my Lambretta scooter driving very slowly and cautiously we reached Jehangir Nursing home and called for Dr. Dalla who had her quarters in the hospital premise on checking up my wife she advised her to stay in a room next to the Delivery thearter instructing a nurse to keep on giving my wife some tablets every half an hour.

In the dead of the night, I had no one to call to in the "Pardesh" so I was sitting out through that cold night on the bench outside that room peeping in occasionally to asses the condition of my wife……. Around 2:30-3 since the nurse in attendance was of a friendly nature she let me sit next to Nishat for the later part of the night which was spent talking in between small naps, around 7:30 that morning the nurse told me to go out of the room as Dr. Dalla was expected anytime, immediately on the arrival of the doctor Nishat was shifted to the delivery room and I kept sitting outside taking a small stroll at intervals around before 8:30 I saw a hospital maid opening the delivery room door charging towards me saying "porga jhala" at first I was confused but on second thought it rang a bell Purga in Marathi means a boy Oh, I was just elated as I had structure the jackpot of my personal life! I took out a ten rupee note and gave it to her as Baksish, then I thanked the Almighty God and the city of Pune for blessing us with a son, the gift for which I can never forget...... the city of Pune through out my life. Remembering veteran Dilip Kumar's song in film Shakti :Maage the ek duva jo kabool ho gaye."

I thanked the Almighty Allah profusely nevertheless, for fulfilling a common man's dream. ValSukrehumdullah......

. ValSubhanallah...

.

.

OVERNIGHT TO DELHI AND BACK

Shri Kanak Trivedi was the Managing director of Gujarat Narmada auto Ltd. a wholly owed subsidiary of GNFC which had taken over GIRNAR scooters. Having joined Girnar scooters a Deputy manager sales and having worked for the Co. for over a year at the time of the takeover Shri Kanak Trivedi the MD had taken a special liking for me and my friend Sanghvi as we were both at the same level of Deputy managers one well versed in Financial aspects of the erst while Co. and other myself in Marketing. During the project stage of GNAL the Co. operated from Odhav Ahmedabad and since there was no selling to done. . Trivedi Saheb utilized my services in planning and in obtaining government licensees for the Scooter project for which I would have to fly down to Delhi a couple of times each month.

One afternoon Trivedi Saheb called me to his cabin around 4 pm and told me that I had to rush down to Delhi on an URGENT …assignment an Italian Automobile designer from Rome had to be received at the DELHI Airport collect the designs besides ensuring he is taken good care of in the best possible manner at the GNFC Nizamudin Guest house thereafter return to Ahmedabad with the designs.

In 1987 since there was just one Indian Airlines flight to Delhi in the evenings from Ahmedabad around 8 pm, I looked at Trivedi Saheb in a questing manner and asked "when sir" "this evening and just now" he said, I was very apprehensive of making it to Delhi on the evening flight as it was a Saturday weekend which could be packed..... Do you mind trying" added Trivedi Saheb, "OK sir, since he was my boss I had to obey his orders and so I immediately rang up our travel agent on returning back to my cabin i.e. Mr. Patel of Goodwind Travels... he told me it was next to impossible, in fact a very bad chance some no. 19 waiting list ticket never the less I told him to book the ticket and keep the return open and as I was just leaving office to collect the ticket and rush to the Airport.

Next I rang up my wife and told her to keep my out station suitcase ready, as I had to go to Delhi on an urgent assignment. This travel bag was always ready at home for in my GNAL project stage period our MD would order us in the middle of the night to reach any weird destination in the shortest period of time.

On reaching Goodwinds at Laldarwaza I asked the auto driver to hold on went inside the Agency collected my tickets and was soon on my way home, on reaching residence I changed (my clothes) collected my suitcase had a quick cup of tea and told my wife that in all probabilities I will be back home by 9::30-10pm as my waitlist no. was 19 and a very bad chance but orders are orders and I have to obey them so wait dinner for me until 10 O'clock atleast.

Being the month of January it started getting chilly by the time I reached the Ahmedabad airport around 7 pm An announcement was made that plus even the flight detail board indicated that the flight was delayed by half an hour..... then it kept on extending. As it started getting colder by the night. I saw a few people presuming them to be waitlist passengers (like me) leaving the airport, I overhead a Gujarati Gentleman telling his wife in the usual loud manner "if Ahmedabad is this cold can you imagine how Delhi will be" The flight landed at 10 that night by which time the mercury could be around 10"C, cold enough for Ahmedabad and so when the waitlist names were called most of them were missing and soon A.G.Mehdi called and Okayed for obtaining a boarding pass for the Delhi flight, I reached Delhi at 12 that night and since the Domestic and International Airport were just adjacent to each other, at that time I hoped on to the international arrival, there I met the GNFC driver with a placard waiting for the Italian gentleman as his flight was to land at 2 am chatting with the driver over a cup of tea from a Tehla stall at the airport entrance and a cigarette the Alitalia flight was heard landing soon.

As the passengers from this flight started trickling out I saw a half bald Italian walk straight towards the driver with our placard before he could reach him I rushed towards him and greeted him by his name and was shocked that he too called me my name perhaps our MD may have informed him! wheeled his suitcase took him to car wait and when our white Ambassador car arrived asked him to get in, during the drive to the GNFC guest house when he spoke he seemed familiar with the progress we had made on the product and the developments at our factory.

On reaching the Nizammudin guest house I ensured he checked in to best room, ordered some coffee and biscuits discussed a few of his experiences at the Piaggo factory collected the drawing and asked him to rest peacefully till the next afternoon as he was to fly to Singapore the next day…. that the driver would take him to the Airport or wherever he desired in the morning as I had no energy left to accompany him.

Getting out of his room around 5:30 in the morning and on reaching the reception counter I banged into Mr. Jittania the Finance Manager of GNFC who was checking out.. he looked at me and we exchanged pleasantries he asked me if I too were checking out, "no no I have just come from Ahmedabad to receive an Italian guest" Trivedi sahib must have sent you"? yes, I said "when are you going back asked Mr. Jattania, I don't know but I have an open air ticket to go back to Ahmedabad. Oh! Then why don't you take a chance as I am going to the airport you can accompany me and since its very cold you stand a good chance, Okay I said and immediately tagged along with him (without checking into the guest house) and to the airport in the car waiting down stairs for him.

On reaching the airport and the airlines counter the ticket collector was only too happy to receive me and give me a boarding pass as on the extremely cold morning at Delhi the flight to Ahmedabad was half empty and the mercury at Delhi had dipped to 6 degrees C.

As soon as the flight took off I dozed off for I had not slept a wink at night to complete my special assignment around 7:15 am the Indian airlines plane touched the Ahmedabad Airport and I got up with the jerk of the thud, I rubbed my eyes and asked Jittania Saheb "where are we? "At Ahmedabad my friend" as soon as we got down I thanked him and bade goodbye into an autorickshaw and reached home within half an hour as the roads were clear on that cold January Sunday morning I rang the doorbell of my house, my wife opened the door after the second buzz looked at me and asked me, "DID you by any chance fall a sleep at the Ahmedabad Airport??? (Kya aap Airport per so gaye the? H ha ha⌡ I laughed and said 'yeh unique experience Trivedi saheb ke naam'....

MISSING THE FLIGHT

During my service with Gujarat Narmada auto Ltd travelling to any destination in India by Air was like jumping on the suburbain train in Bombay during college days.

Having shifted to the GNFC colony at Bharuch known as Narmadanagar from Ahmedabad when the factory at Valia was completed it so happened that our MD Shri Kanak Trivedi along with my colleague Shri Sanghvi had to reach Delhi for some conference called by the GNFC North Zone before the introduction of the final scooter 'Narmada prince' in the market.

Trivedi Saheb called me as usual to his cabin at Valia and told me to book the air tickets for himself, Sanghvi and my self to Delhi by the evening flight from Baroda on a particular day later that week. Incidentally, in the year 1987-88 the Indian airlines Baroda-Delhi evening flight was 6 days in week but the departure timings every alternate day were different i.e. 8 pm Monday, 9 pm Tuesday then again 8 pm Wed. and so on, some difference of an hour every alternate day.

Having booked the tickets through our travel agent Cox and king's I was under the impression of an 9 pm flight that evening and informed my MD and Sanghvi accordingly without confirming with the agent.

When staying at Narmada Nagar Bharuch we had to drive down to Baroda which took an hour and a half to reach the Chani airport at Baroda, hence I planned to leave for the 9 pm flight and informed the MD's driver accordingly to pick Sanghvi and myself from our quarters before driving up to the bosses residence just before leaving home and collecting the ticket for keeping them in my pouch I browsed the tickets only to find to my utter dismay that the departure was of 8 pm and not 9 pm as I had perceived and informed all concerned.

On noticing this mistake I panicked as MD Trivedi sahib had checked the same with me at the office and I had confirmed it as a 9 O'Clock flight.

Luckily as soon as I realized this massive error the driver rang my door bell to collect me I rushed out and told him to bring Sanghvi Saheb at once as I had got the departure time wrong Sanghvi joined us and I told him of this mistake he too froze for a while for he knew that Trivedi sahib would blow his top for learning this mistake.

Never the less, I said my prayers and was hoping against hope that the flight be delayed in arriving so that the departure too stands delayed as was the case in many of our journeys from Baroda to Delhi.

Trivedi sahib too was ready when we reached his house and soon we had hit the high way towards Baroda. I was sitting in the front with the driver Rakesh

Chauhan and Sanghvi was sitting in the rear with the MD discussing some financial aspects of the company, many a time they would ask me for my opinion from the marketing point of view and I would answer in just HU Hah as my total concentration was to reach Baroda airport in time and collect the boarding pass.

Rakesh was driving faster than usual but since Trivedi sahib was involved in a discussion he did not shout at him to slow down, however my stars were bad that day and soon we ran into a highway jam caused by some accident losing some 15 minutes in it thereby nullifying all the back log Rakesh had recovered by driving at his best.

Whilst approaching Baroda we saw the plane land at the Chani airport but by the time we actually reached the airport the counter had closed, I ran with the tickets to the airport Managers cabin and barged into it, since I was a regular he let me in I told him the whole story of mistaking the departure and was pleading with him to let us board the plane pitting me perhaps he spoke to the captain in the cockpit of the plane who said that the doors were ordered to be locked and that he just count help, I once again pleaded with him to just allow one passenger in, my MD will miss an important meeting.

I don't recollect but maybe I was almost on my knees requesting and pleading, when I felt someone place a hand over my shoulder, I turned around and realized it was Trivedi sahib my MD standing with his hand on my shoulder and just when I thought he would shout and blow me up saying you are fired Mr. Mehdi, he looked at me very lovingly and said aloud "stop begging like that you have not committed a murder, actually since yesterday I didn't feel like going for this meeting good we have missed the flight, come lets go to a good restaurant have dinner and go home peacefully", then he turned around to Sanghvi (who was flabbergasted to note the anticlimax reaction of Trivedi sahib) who too was now standing in the managers cabin, call Delhi R.M. and tell him we are not coming (to Delhi) he finally apologized to the manager for the scene created in his room and added that I count bear to see my "chukoro" begging and pleading he did make a mistake about the departure time but I am sure it was not intentional, the manager felt sorry that he could not help and we left the airport.

After ordering dinner at the Kwality restaurant at Baroda Trivedi sahib pushed off to the wash room Sanghvi then broke his silence and told me that it was only the fatherly love which the MD has for us which saved you, had it been someone else he would blasted him to pieces.

The moral of the story is to always as certain the (departure) timings on ones tickets and work dedicatedly to create a bond of selfless love and affection even at the work place that even a strictest boss like Trivedi Saheb is ready to forgive.

HASMUKH'S DISMISSAL OR REINSTATMENT ?

After the takeover by GNFC of GIRNAR scooters alongwith the staff who desired to stay on were initially asked to report on duty at the odhav office Ahmedabad it was during the project stage itself that the shifting and transfer to Valia in Ankleshwar commenced, hence the personnel as and when required were transferred one by one with allocation of residential quarters at the Narmadanagar township of GNFC.

In this process, I being the head of the Sales department was also asked to shift to Narmananagar Bhauch alongwith my sales and service engineer team, which also included persons such as Hasmukh Vandra sales Assistant Sailesh Gandhi sales Accountant and Prajapati the General assistant who were so faithful (to me) that if I asked them to jump out of a running train they would do that without questioning why, sir?

To conduct the initial survey on the customer profile of the product being prepared made as a scooter (in the market) we were giving an "A" class quarter at Narmadanagar township as a transit office of the Sales deptt and so I along with my sales team started work at this place where as the production, technical purchase, finance personnel and administration departments were asked to start work in temporary offices at the factory premises at Valia. MD Shri Trivedi sahib also started holding his office at valia and whenever he needed advice on sales aspects I was called to go down to valia from Narmadanagar Township.

During these days some customer records shifted from odhav were lying in my chamber and I had asked Hasmukh Vandra my sales assistant to open these records and draw up a mailing list of customers with whom we could correspond and receive some feed back on the performance of the product they had used i.e.the Girnar scooter through which improvements could be suggested for the new product being developed. Hasmukh my assistant kept on postponing complining this list for over a month where as I kept on reminding him almost every alternate day and he would assure me that within a day or two he would finish the task and give the mailing list. MD sahib had also cross checked with me on this issue a couple of times and I in turn had passed on the same assurance to him.

One day it so happened that our Advertising company Mundra asked me for this data as they preparing the Advertising campaign for the product to be launched this was because MD had instructed Mundra to collect the same from me.

Knowing Trivedi saheb's nature I panicked as the process of the list of customers to be complied and letters sent with a free answer envelope and the reply to be received and than the feedback to be given would atleast consume a minimum of 8 to 10 days, hence I called Hasmukh to my cabin and asked him to leave all other work but furnish me this data by evening without giving me any excuses or assurances.

Hasmukh was a person with no or limited rationals and so he once again took it lightly I warned him to take it seriously so he assured me once again that it will be on my table the next day. The next morning this data was upmost on my mind so on reaching office I first checked up for the same on finding the work not done I called Hasmuskh and told him to start this assignment immediately Hasmukh perhaps was not in the best of moods and so he replied it cannot be done today. I lost my cool and I shouted at him saying why did you keep on promising me that it will be done and now what answer will I give to Mudra and the MD he curtly retorted that's its not his lookout.... this made me more furious. So I told him either you do this job or leave the job and so he said I would rather resign, well then give me your papers and in the heat of the moment he did that.

I kept his resignation with me till lunch hoping he will cool down realise his mistake and start doing the job but there was no sign of remorse, so I called him again to my cabin after lunch and threatened him that I will go to valia and hand it over the management for execution, but he just replied do as you please.

This attitude of defiance was enough for me to call for the company car and rush down to valia at the MD's office wih his resignation on reaching valia I narrated the whole story to the MD who also reacted in a furious manner called the Manager personnel and asked him to accept Hasmukh's resignation with immediate effect settle his dues and pack him off at the earliest before close of office hours, his acceptance letter was typed and handed over to me to carry it back to Narmadanagar Bharuch.

I left the valia office with a heavy heart I knew Hasmulh was one of my loyal subordinates but could not understand his weird behaviour.

However, on reaching my quaters at the Transit lounge building, Narmadanagar my wife asked me to have my bath after which dinner was served over she questioned me " what have you done today? Something……. I never expected of you" she said, 'what is that now' I asked her, "you have stepped on the job of one of your subordinates, he is a poor man with a family to support how could you have done that!" I felt very guilty as on second thought I too felt that I had over reacted.

Anyway, how did you know this I asked her? she then told me that the whole department had come down to the house after office hours along with Hasmukh and told me that what had happened Hasmukh then told her that "saab" I thought would tear my resignation but God knows he reacted differently and carried it to valia.

On learning this I really felt sorry for what I had done just then the door bell rang and on opening it ,I saw all the members of my sales department standing at the entrance along with Hasmukh Vandra, who on seeing me apologized for his adamant behavior.

I called them in, a group of 8 to 10 person had a cup of tea with them and assured them of my reverse action, that night I could not sleep well and my wifes words and Hasmukh's apology kept ringing in my ears, next morning I called the driver and asked him to take me to the MD's office at valia, Trivedi sheb on seeing me in his office in the morning was not at all surprised he received me with a smile and told me that " if I know you well enough I was sure that I will return with the company's resignation acceptance letter of Hasmukh" in fact , he added "you have perhaps come with apology letter too from Hasmukh".

No, I said then call him here and take it first to enable us to reverse all the paperwork, this was done immediately and I was saved from the sin of firing a poor loyal man who even today keeps on reciting this episode saying that "If there ever has to be saab under whom one should work he should be like Mehdi Saab."

On recollecting this episode, I always   attribute it to the attitude of empathy which I had perhaps developed which was inherited from my late father who was my ideal in many walks of life.

INDIAN UNDER THE BRITISH

It was in the year 1987-88 after the takeover of GIRNAR scooters by the GNFC at Bharuch that the new plant which was technically a state of the art one an extremely improved product a geared scooter was developed at the Valia, the scooter subsidiary company was named Gujarat Narmada Auto Ltd and when an appropriate name for the new product was being discussed. The advertising company of GNFC i.e. Mudra communications thought of advertising a name the product contest with a slogan which would also create the required awareness of the new scooter when it would be launched at the National level.

Thousand of applications were received in "The name the product context" and finally the product was named as "Narmada Prince" an advertising campaign and film by Mudra was also finalized and the product was ready to be launched in the National market.

Since, I was the head of the Sales department of GNAL all functions connected with marketing of the product i.e. The market survey, Advertising organizing the service Department excetra were assigned to me but when the ultimate product was ready to be launched in the market GNFC the holding company insisted that their Fertilizer marketing team could to the job and that there was no need to recruit a separate sales team by the scooter subsidiary.

Trivedi saheb our MD differed on this issue for he very well knew that marketing Fertilizers in the rural area was a different ball game to selling scooters in major cities and towns of urban India, however in a Board meeting called for the purpose of finalizing this decision he could not have his way as most of the Directors were basically from GNFC and were in favour of the GNFC team marketing the product.

This decision had put me off to a great extent as all my dreams of heading an All India marketing team were shattered and was left with no choice but to reconcile to the fact of working under the instructions of GNFC marketing department, right from the beginning of this arrangement I felt choked for their total concept and attitude from the time of selecting a dealer to the ultimate marketing of the product was different and smacked of rural over tones.

Secondly since the GNAL factory and housing colony were at valia a backward area in Bharuch district I was forced to send back my family to Ahmedabad for want of good English medium schools nearby, hence though I was allotted the best of residential quarters at valia. I had no choice but to go down to Ahmedabad every weekend and come back to valia every Monday spend the week here at work then again go back to Ahmedabad at weekends this went on for about a year and my peaceful family life was totally disturbed.

Finally, the behavior and attitude of the GNFC personnel towards the GNAL employees and staff was indicating an attitude of over lordship for they considered us as parasites and openly exhibited it whenever the occasion arose,the superiority complex of the GNFC kept on growing as time went on and soon a number of officers including myself started feeling that it would be better to opt-out rather than slog here without being acknowledged

Hence, I seriously started searching for an appropriate alternate openings in the Automobile industry and having got one put in my papers at valia but Trivedi saheb my MD tore my resignation and convinced me to have patience and stay back for sooner or later he was hopeful of the marketing activities being transferred or ultimately given to GNAL.

Time went on and instead of passing on the marketing of scooters to GNAL the GNFC marketing team were convinced that they were doing a fantastic job of marketing the product which was many a time seen lying side by side fertilizers bags at mofussil outlets of dealers who worked as common outlets for the sales of the fertilizers and the scooters of GNFC, this shabby manner of display and sales of a product developed with so much pain and perseverance was too much for me to digest as a marketing man from the automobile industry.

The shunting to Ahmedabad at weekends and back also went on for about a year and once again due to some hassel with the GNFC overlords I put in my resignation but my MD Trivedi saheb once again found a way of retaining me and transferred me to the Ahmedabad GNFC office to look after the service department of the scooters sold in Gujarat and help the GNFC marketing team on sales of the product in the Gujarat market.

Though not too happy I worked at the GNFC Ahmedabad office for over a year and at last I managed to obtain a good offer from M/s. Kinetic Honda ltd as an Area manager either at U.P. Punjab or Bihar and obviously my choice was U.P. as the Khalistan movement was at its peak in Punjab at that time and Bihar was a underdeveloped state though no terrorist movement existed there the Goonda Raj was worse than the Khalajhan movement!

Having this opportunity up my sleeve I convinced Shri Desai Saheb who was RM GNFC Gujarat to please get my resignation accepted by MD Trivedi Saheb and releave me from GNAL to enable me enhance my career in the Automobile Industry even if it were outside Gujarat. Shri Desai Saheb understood my anxiety and promised to help me in this endeavor, perhaps he had gauged my potential and released that I was wasting my time here playing second fiddle to the GNFC fertilizer marketing staff.

As luck would have it within the next 2 or 3 days after the submission of my resignation for the third time Trivedi Saheb was to visit the Ahmedabad office …and finally the day came, perhaps after the normal market report or feedback from Shri Desai Saheb he must have forwarded my resignation and requested him to accept it as I was very keen to be releaved, pat rang the bell and I was summoned in to the chamber.

Trivedi saheb looked at me from top to TOE for he LIKED me as a person immensely and could not digest the thought of my leaving his company, so he asked me very bluntly Mehdi just give me one good reason and your answer in one line why you wish to leave the company.… if I am convinced I will let you go. I hesitated for a while and quietly replied, "Sir, I feel like an Indian under the British"….. he froze for while but I knew I had convinced him he mummered something in pain signed my resignation and walked out of the office.

A DESPERATE EFFORT

Year 1988 and 1989

Having joined Kinetic engineering Ltd as an Area manager in U.P. state with headquarters at Lucknow,it was my solemn duty and responsibility to build a good team of Sales executives for the Regional office thereby enhance sales of the Kinetic Luna and Kinetic Honda scooter in the state of U.P. and build a strong image of the company and the product which lacked prominence as at that time competitive products of TVS, Bajaj and Hero were doing fairly well in that state.

Slowly but gradually even Kinetic Honda as a scooter started getting accepted as a product in the fairly orthodox markets of Lucknow, Allahabad, Varanasi, Agra, Meerut, Aligarh, Bareilly etcetra.

To encourage the sales team for obtaining better results the company had worked out and formulated some target incentive schemes on quarterly and annual basis, one such scheme was coming to an end when I was on tour with one of my sales executives covering the Aligarh, Agra, Bareilly belt by the name of Rajan, after working for the day at Aligarh I was to travel back to Lucknow by the Gomti express, however Rajan was marginally falling short of achieving his incentive number and he hoped to achieve it from the Bareilly dealer Oberoi Motors, when Rajan informed me about this I told him not to worry as I had an excellent relations with Mr. Oberoi and on reaching Lucknow will phone him to place the order with him to complete his target requirement, however Rajan was not convinced and wanted me to personally call on Mr. Oberoi at Bareilly as that would carry the required weight and he would not refuse placing the order for Oberoi Motors which was sufficiently stocked and had refused to place the order with Rajan during his last visit.

To fulfill my duty as a caring manager I reluctantly agreed to stay back at Aligarh, catch the morning U.P. SRTC bus to Bareilly along with Rajan get him the required order to complete his shortfall and reach back home at Lucknow the next evening.

The next morning around 8 am as planned we caught the early morning super express bus to Bareilly, all was well until we reached the outskirts of Badaun a Tehsil town of Bareilly district at a police check post at around 11 am after some discussion of the conductor with the police all passenger were informed that the bus will not go further due to the communal riots which have broken out at Badaun one may leave the bus and proceed to his destination on his own or remain seated as the bus would go back to Aligarh,

Hearing this announcement Rajan was very disturbed I told him that its better to go back to Aligarh and I would request Mr. Oberoi to give him the order to complete the target but he was restless went out and found out that from the railway station of this suburb a train was due to arrive which would proceed to Bareilly through via Badaun.

He forced me once again not to refuse but get into this train and somehow reach Bareilly. However, we got off the bus hired a pedal rickshaw and reached this station, the name of which I cannot recall.

The train arrived and we got into the first class compartment which was almost empty hence were happy that very soon we will be at Bareilly and perhaps more comfortably then in a bus. No sooner we entered Badaun we were soon surrounded with the noise fire and turmoil which had erupted in there,,I vividly remember the scenes of chaos which alarmed both Rajan and myself and our peaceful idea of reaching Bareilly stood cancelled. At Badaun station when the train stopped a huge wave of panicked persons entered the compartment and soon the first class coach looked more like a second class compartment of the Bombay suburb train of peak hours.

After an halt of about 15 minutes the train left the Badaun station only to stop after a couple of minutes due to some chain pulling. Then started once again covered a kilometer or two and stopped once again, this place looked quite rural, however just then we saw some villagers with their faces covered with turban and with huge sticks in their hands knocking on the outer side of the coaches announcing very loudly and clearly that "All Hindus should a light from the train and all muslims should remain back inside the train" on hearing this a lot of people panicked including Rajan and myself a number of thoughts ran through my mind in a fraction of a second and fearing the worst of setting the whole train on fire after the hindus alight I too picked up my bag to get down, Rajan seemed confused as he was a hindu and I was a muslim, I gazed at him and told him in a whispser "please don't call my name as you are in the habit of repeating "Mehdi saheb" I am also taking a chance and getting down and now lets go we both got down and ran towards a lane through the fields just then two villagers appeared with sticks in their hands and cautioned us to take the other lane on the left side as this one lead up to a muslim village, this diversion alarmed me even more and I thought my time has come let me say my prayers for the moment I reach the hindu village I maybe slaughtered in the mean time a number of muslims too got down from the train and as soon as they were identified 4 villager would surround them and punch the stick one after the other on the head of the person who would collapse with his skull broken into pieces. I having seen atleast 10 collapse in that manner infact one of them was a Burkha lady accompanied by a small child.

In this commotion may be from the blues a God sent police jeep suddenly appeared, the police got down and fired a few shots in the air and announced on the megaphone that no one should move and should go back to the train which will in turn will go back to Badaun railway station. I took a deep breath and stood still for a while looked up thanked the Almighty and my stars for this close call, moved back to the train and climbed up the nearest coach on the way back I saw those innocent all lying in a pool of blood probably dead for no fault of theirs the lady in the burkha was also dead with her small daughter next to the body and crying as they had spared the child.

On climbing up the train I saw yet another scene I will never forget there was this muslim lady who was shivering with fright to such an extent that it seemed she was performing some kind of jurk dance we tried to pacify her and it took atleast some good 8 to 10 minutes before she stopped shivering and then started sobbing in loud bursts it seemed she was terribly shocked with all that was happenings in and around her.

The train atlast started moving back towards Badaun and we reached the platform within the next few minutes ,the streets and sound while approaching the town and the station were chaotic and a petrol pump just next to the station was up in flames.

A number of injured were being brought to the station on stretchers and the whole town as far as we could see was full of turmoil and smoke, ,. on getting down I quietly walked to a vacant bench and Rajan sat down next to me we sat frozen for almost an hour then Rajan gathered some courage and told me that he was very sorry for dragging me into this mess he then added that he felt extremely frightened as he had never seen such scenes in his life, I consoled him by saying that I was equally petrified as I had just overcome a very close call in the outskirts of the town, we then got up went to the water tap drank some water came back and sat on the same place just then we saw some officials walk into the station masters room and a small crowd following them. Rajan was curious to know what was happening so he got up and joined the group soon,I saw him waveing towards me calling me to also join the "Tamasha" when I reached him I saw the District Magistrate speaking in the station master's wireless system perhaps to the Police head quarters at Bareilly, (since all the telephone lines in the town had gone dead) saying something like the situation in the town is in control and you need not worry as there is no need for additional reinforcement, just then the Station master snatched the wireless phone from the D.M. and said I am the Station master of Badaun on the line, sir, the situation here today is out of control please rush additional police force here, the D.M. is trying to save his chair and has given a wrong report, he then put down the instrument turned to the D.M. and lashed out at him saying he would be held responsible for all the additional deaths which take place in the riots today, please leave my chamber, sir and don't play with lives of innocent people just to save your chair.

The D.M. seemed utterly embarrassed but didn't say anything, as he knew the Station master was absolutely right he walked out of the room alongwith his orderlies we too walked out went and sat on the same bench the evening had decended on Badaun railway station but the admiration for the Station master by the name Vermaji or Sharmaji kept on growing in my heart to such an extent that after the rush had cleared I could not resist my feelings, got up and walked towards this great man's chamber, Rajan followed me I went into his room he was sitting quite alone doing some work on his table looked up at us and gestured as to what do we want? nothing I said sir, I have just come to salute you for the great act you have committed towards humanity today many may or may not say so but to me you are a Great man and a Hero he smiled and told us additional police force is on its way to Badaun from Bareilly, Rajan soon butted in, when is this train leaving to Bareilly? he said it will leave as soon as the additional police force comes.

The train left at some time after 10 pm that night we reached Bareilly nonstop by midnight got down and thanked God once again with a sigh of relief. Rajan was almost back to normal and asked me to stay over once again in some hotel for the night calling on the dealer next morning, but by now my patience had run out and I curtly told him that I will catch the next train to Lucknow please let me go I will telephone Mr. Oberoi and he will definitely oblige us. Rajan knew that this episode had shattered me, he ran towards the ticket window bought me a ticket for Lucknow for the Delhi mail which was due to arrive shortly.

On reaching Lucknow and attending the office the next day I had a message waiting for me on my table from Rajan at Bareilly it read:- "Mr. Oberoi has given the target order after hearing our effort in desperation (story) sorry, for all that happened yesterday and thank you for being such a great and loving boss! Sales Officer Rajan salutes Area Manager Mehdi saheb"......

THE RATH YATRA ?

It was in the year 1989 that the Rath Yatra for constructing Ram mandir at Ayodhya was undertaken by Shri L.K. Advani from Porbander in Gujarat to Ayodhya in U.P. The journey has made history as it was very successful in establishing the BJP as a political force in the country, at the same time collecting crores of rupees in the name of establishing a Ram temple and later in bringing down the 350 year old Babri Masjid perceived by many as a symbol of Muslims/ Mughal rule which this school of thought claims was built at the birth place of Lord Shri Ram Chandra.

To cut the long story short the BJP as a political force was making desperate efforts for obtaining power on the Ram mandir issues which could be solved amicably from the very first day still hangs in abeyance dividing the country on communal lines filling the coffers of this political party besides enhancing its vote bank.

It was during the famous Rath Yatra days that I managed a change of job from U.P. back to Gujarat on promotion as Deputy Regional Manager to enhance the sales of Hero puch a new two wheeler launched in the market by the Hero Group of companies.

Since the new job offered me an opportunity to go back to Gujarat my home state with a better remuneration package I accepted it and booked my tickets back to

Ahmedabad along with the family. Shahzadi my daughter was 12 years then and Jehangir my son foundly called "Baba" was around 9. the entire family had taken a liking to Lucknow because of its culture, education and the locality where we were resided i.e Indiranagar and were finding it difficult to leave the city of the Nawabs and breakdown of bonds with such loving neighbours. Just at this time the rath yatra journey was abruptly stopped by Shri Lalu Prasad Yadav in Bihar before it could reach U.P. and Ayodhya as the Mad "Hindutva" hipe was growing regularly and this incident proved to be an anticlimax to a much talked about climax which was planned by the BJP, however this famous arrest brought in a lot of trouble from the very next day as communal riots broke out all over the country including Lucknow and parts of U.P.

Travel services by rail and road were immediately discontinued specially towards Lucknow and Ayodhya to stop the inflow of Karsevaks at the disputed site however, we had booked out tickets back home to Ahmedbad much in advance to the chaotic situation by Sabarmati Express, which also stood cancelled.

Having resigned from Kinetic Engineering at Lucknow, I was given a dead line by Hero Motors to join my new assignment at Ahmedabad, hence could not take a chance in delaying or cancelling the journey to Ahmedabad and reporting for joining the new job in time.

News of the communal flareups kept on increasing everyday and curfew was imposed in all major towns of U.P., M.P. and Gujarat the route through which Sabarmati goes back to Ahmedabad at one stage we were even contemplating travelling back by air with the entire family but as we were carrying a lot of luggage and there being no direct flight from Lucknow to Ahmedabad, we dropped the idea.

During the course of these dreadful days we kept on packing our articles and bags to take back home quite religiously, it so happened one fine day when I was packing one of the wooden boxes, one old lady of the neighborhood i.e. Indiranagar A block, where we stayed happened topass by our house and heard he knocking on the wood of my sealing the box and just casually questioned as to what I was up to? just for a little fun I jokingly replied to this aunty Dixit, "Being afraid we intend to run away from this place", "why so" she asked, "because there are only two muslim families surrounded by some 100 hindu houses. The answer really agitated her and she lost her cool she shouted back at the top of her voice in the lane, how dare you say that, no one can even touch you in this lane, how dare you say that, no one can even touch you in this lane, how can you think of saying such a thing. My wife came running out of the house to pacify her for she knew the neighborhood and the entire locality loves us so much that we could not been on a safer place in such troubled times.

After a couple of days the situation in U.P. started cooling down a bit but the other states including Gujarat was bad, however Sabarmati was reintroduced as the U.P. government wanted the Kersevaks to return back to their homes from Ayodhya. In all this commotion and with the curfew still prevailing the departure day arrived and we ultimately decided to catch the train back to Ahmedabad, hence the 3 closest neighbours the Avasthes, the Kumars and the Ganguars and their families made arrangement for curfew passes and came to see us off at the Lucknow station.

Reaching the Lucknow station first they took our names off the reservation chart then they went and bought a Mangasutra and sindoor for my wife and sternly warned my son not to call his sister "Aapi" but "Didi" in the train. They helped us book our luggage in the luggage bogey and stuffed our compartment with immediate utility items. Luckily the cabin allotted to us was for four passenger hence we were instructed to stay indoors as much as possible and only go out to the toilet. They packed us with tiffins and food brought from the respective homes which could last us for more than two days so that we need not venture out even for food.

The train finally left at around midnight instead of the evening and they all stayed back till it left the platform and their faces burled, before the final announcement, I cannot forget the honest good byes of my neighbours and the sobs of their wives clinging on to my wife as if saying adieu to their real own sister, who can ever say that we were muslims and they were hindus in a country which was burning and torn apart with manmade communal hatred?

The entire journey from Lucknow to Ahmedabad is still fresh and vivid in my mind as the train was full of Karsevaks returning or shunted back from Ayodhya. They would get down at every major station stand in a que and utter slogans such as "Hum Mandir WaheBanaige" etcetra ,etcetra.

However, we managed to reach Ahmedabad on the second morning at around 8:30 am never the less on reaching Ahmedabad we were informed that this city too was under curfew, somehow we managed to off load ourselves and on leaving the platform we were encountered by a number of Autorickshaw drivers ready to ferry us across the curfewed city but the moment we announced our destination they would leave us alone and runaway, on probing deeper with a friendly looking auto driver who happened to be a muslim we were informed that Sarkhej road being a muslim inhabitant the hindu drivers were not willing to take a chance, besides we were travelling with a lot of luggage and one auto would not suffice, thus we were now confronted with the task of locating two muslim auto drivers, one was already there and after a great search managed the second one.. ....m mn our way back I got into one rickshaw with my daughter and in the other was my wife with my son, soon our station to home journey commenced and on the way back a number of questions about the intensity of the riots were answered by the auto drivers then as Nishat my wife informs me her auto driver whilst nearing Paldi looked at her very surprisingly and asked her if she was a muslim and whose house were we going to? she replied very empathetically that she is a pure Mughlani and that the address given is that of her father Janab Mirza saheb, is that so questioned the auto driver then why are you wearing a mangal sutra and sindoor in your hair which can be very detrimental once we enter that area and could lead a muslim to mistake you for a hindu lady, so for Gods sake please take it off once we enter the Juhapura area, to ensure your safety! My wife on hearing this immediately complied and by God's grace and the best wishes of both the hindus and muslims we covered a journey of 1100 kilometres in the thick of the Rath Yatra riots, surely a journey not in a Rath but in a train the Sabarmati express we cannot forget.

This unfortable journey is also a Q.E.D. to all concerned that the country cannot and will not be divided just by pulling down Masjids and building temples at its site ? be it today or in the future. ..

.

THE LION WAS NO MORE

After returning back from Lucknow to Ahmedabad from the two and half year stint with Kinetic Engineering as its Area manager I joined Hero motors as a Deputy regional manager looking after Gujarat to promote and propell the sales of "Heropuch". This new assignment gave me an opportunity to gather and renew my contacts in Ahmedabad and Gujarat again. The first few months were spent in surveying and appointing new dealers in places unrepresented, infact most of the dealers of sister products such as Hero majestic and Hero Honda were only too happy to accept the Hero puch dealership a small vehicle of 65 cc but with a lot of power.

Shradha motors at Ahmedabad was my Head quarters and Mr. Rajender Seth its owner soon became a very good friend, however during the course of my tours and travels to promote the product I made it a point to find sometime after duty hours to meet my old colleagues of GNAL and it was in one of those meetings at Surat that I was informed by Mr. Suryaanarayan C. A. of GNAL about the where about of Trivedi Saheb my ex-MD who always loved me like a son.

As the story told to me by Mr, Suryanarayanan Trivedi Saheb too had quit GNAL and joined Reliance as a CEO at Hazira he was then assigned the task of developing the entire Jamnagar project of Reliance refinery it was during this stage that cancer of the throat was detected on him. The company Reliance had even sent him to Japan for treatment but the dreaded disease had got the better of him and was in its final stage hence no amount of treatment could save him and that his days were limited.

Learning of this sad condition of a person from who I had learnt a lot I desired to meet him at least one before he left us for good hence, Suryanarayanan informed me that he had finally shifted to his farm house at Wakaner a town a few miles from Rajkot where I should meet him for he always remembered me   and would fondly recall my crazy episodes of GNAL. (Missing the flight, Dismissal of Hasmukh etc…….)

The very next week, I planned a trip to Rajkot and on finishing work that evening asked the new dealer appointed there Shri Balbhadra Chudasma to help me reach Wakaner as I desperately wanted to pay my last respects to a man I considered a Lion in all respect be it the field of Administration, Marketing or Human personal relationships.

Hence, the next morning we jumped in to his car and were soon on our way to Wakaner on reaching Wakaner Balbhadra had some contacts there through who we managed to locate Trivedi saheb's farm house a place few minutes away from the town. Finally on reaching the Gates of his dwelling I had a smile on my face perhaps the satisfaction of meeting my great mentor. A few meters from the gate was his single storey farm house at the entrance of which I spoted his son who recognized me, we got down from the car and he greeted us and took us into the house there I greeted his wife and daughters and a few other family members. They all seemed very quite asked me If I desired to have a cup of tea, which I consented to. They then told me in Gujarati that saheb has gone upstairs. There was a lot of silence all around and I presumed that it existed because of the stage of his illness. A few minutes later the tea was served to us in between the silence his son asked me about my family and the new job and as to how I managed to reach here; it was almost an hour since I had reached this place and was getting restless to meet Trivedi saheb, I looked up at the house a couple of times and wandered as to what a sickman would be doing up there on the terrace in such a precarious state of health?

Having lost control my patience I finally told, his son that if saheb cannot come down I don't mind going up....... to meet him? its then that his son broke and told me that by up he meant that he had passed away just 2 days ago. This was too much for me to swallow as I had come with great hopes of meeting him for the last time, hence I broke down and (which I have rarely done in my professional career) all those seated in and around also started crying. I then got up folded my hands and addressed his family. I had come down with great hopes of meeting the Lion but unfortunately 'the Lion was no more.......'

MY GREATEST MISTAKE

It was from October 1990 around Diwali times to October 1995 that I worked for Hero motors initially as a deputy Regional manager than as a Manager Marketing looking after the interest of the company in Gujarat, during this period I was stationed at Ahmedabad as the H.Q. Town and operated my activities from Shradha Motors the Ahmedabad main dealer.

The owner of Shradha Motors though on paper was Mrs Nita Seth the defacto proprietor was her husband Shri Rajender Seth, hence before proceeding further it will be in place to brief you on the family back ground of on one of the best couple I have worked with in my long years of association within the automobile industry, incidently shri Rajender Seth is non other than the son-in-law of Shri O P. Munjal the vice chairman of the Hero Group of companies and Chairman Hero cycles certainly a name to reckon with in the private sector industries of our country.

Inspite of belonging to this elite business back ground Raju bhai today is one of my best friends and though we have not worked together since over 20 years it seems only yesterday that we were together. Being stationed as a company Manager to lookafter the marketing of the products of Hero motors in Gujarat our business association soon grew into a personal friendship. Looking back and analyzing the reason for this relationship are perhaps certain factors which were in common between us.

We belonged to the same age group and had spent our childhood in a common city Bombay hence our social environment matched to a very great extent, including our period of schooling and graduation he at Jaihind and I at Xaviers besides his love for Hindi music and mine were quite similar which only helped to build a quick understanding on all aspects.

Coming down to work and its ethics Raju bhai believed in working hard to promote the product he sold which again was a factor of common link hence we soon started understanding and getting along with each other very easily.

However, his quality of salesmanship of detailing the product to an any unknown prospective buyer was so convincing and friendly that I have seen him his hand around the neck of prospective buyers and explain the plus points of the product as if to a long time buddy! Besides his P.R. and playing host is par excellence for if you known him a little and happen to call on him you are sure to be treated to the best snacks and beverages available around his showroom. This attribute urges me to confess very candidly that during my tenure of 5 years with the company I was never allowed to eat outside whilst visiting Shradha Motors, infact I was told by

Raju Bhai from the very first day of office that every afternoon I will have to have lunch with him and will not carry my lunch or tiffin from my home.....now thats called hospitality and I don't feel the least ashamed in accepting the fact that every afternoon on a working day in Ahmedabad at Shradha Motors for a period of 5 years religiously my lunch alongwith his huge tiffin box came from his residence or was sent to Shradha motors that means every month atlest 10 days in a month I was his official guest...?

During the course of these 5 years though academically I was a qualified Marketing man I learnt a lot from him in acquiring practical experience of projecting and advertising a product in the local media, be it the press, radio or a leaflet, this lead me to project him as a "Role Model dealer" to the entire dealer network in Gujarat during my visit to their stations. He on the other hand as the feedback goes would talk about my commitment sincerity and dedication to the cause of the company not only to the Dealer fatemity but the senior Managers of the company. This mutual understanding and admiration for each other just kept on growing which made us operate on the same wave length and Hero motor along with Shradha motors may not have seen better days as far as I recollect in terms of enhanced sales and goodwill of their products at Ahmedabad.

However, I personally harboured no such intensions and was focused on only doing my duties to the best of my ability.

Since the head office of Hero motors was at New Delhi and the Executive Director Shri Pankaj Munjal Saheb was the brother-in-law of Shri Raju Bhai Seth the senior managers of the company always nursed a surpressed anxiety fearing that all the praise Raju Bhai showered on me may lead me to acquire a senior position in the Marketing Department of the H.O. in future.

In such an atmosphere, one such G.M. Marketing wanted to destabilize my progress so during one of the All India Marketing conferences at Delhi (somewhere in September 1995) he called me on one side and told me aside. ... that being pleased with my results in Gujarat the company wished to promote me by offering me a senior position in the All India Marketing of spare parts of the product from the factory. I thanked him formally but questioned the reason of my promotion to the Spare parts department when I had been instrumental in increasing vehicle sales? to which he had no answer??

Having sensed a punishment transfer I requested him to give me some time near February / March when I could come down with my family and not disturb their schooling or education of my children, he willingly agreed to this request and assured me to honour it, however, on reaching Ahmedabad back from the conference I was informed by one of my well wishers in the Delhi H.O. that my immediate transfer orders were being typed.

This information upset me for though the G.M. had agreed to my request, he had double crossed me by actually learning of my anxiety and playing on it. Raju Bhai understood that the G.M. was playing games and urged me to accept the transfer but I was so upset that I refused to budge and instead put in my papers hoping the Management will call me to Delhi and ask me to explain the reason for such an extreme step, but the contarary happened for I presume the schrewd G.M. had already briefed E.D. saheb about my reaction and hence my resignation stood accepted. It was Diwali time when I stood relieved from the services of the company having served it for 5 years. This was probably the biggest mistake of my life for which I cannot forgive myself even today.

However, what was destined cannot be waived, never the less these 5 years gave me an opportunity to study the reason why the Munjals have grown so fast as a Business house and the secret of their success which is simply the letter "Love" it is the art of building a personal bond or relationship with all who work with them, whether in the capacity of a dealer or an employee making them feel that you care for them and their family. I have had the good fortune of personally seeing Shri O.P. Munjal saheb and Shri B.M. Lal saheb addressing press conferences and mamoth Dealer meets and accepting candidly how they started life after partition making cycle parts and hawking it all over Punjab....... then assembling their own cycles graduating to manufacturing and becoming the largest producers of cycles in the entire world subsequently venturing into production of the famous Hero mopeds and clenching the collaboration with Honda Motors of Japan and creating History by giving the developing Indian economy the most feul efficient motor cycle the Hero Honda CD-100.... how can one forget the immortal slogan or caption to promote this product "The Fill it, forget it: byke.

It was in these formative years that the Hero group allotted the Motor cycle dealership preferably to their cycle dealers who grew a long with them and can never desert them as the bond of personal relationship has now grown over a couple of generation and can never die.

I have worked for the Flrodia group as Area Manager UP for Kinetic Engineering Ltd an also as a Branch Manager Cama Motors handling Bajaj Auto 2 wheeler dealership at Gandhinagar and have seen all the Big names in the Automobile group but the personal bond love and affection the Munjals and their officials shower on you in any capacity is far too superior and the reason of their unending success.

Its been 15 years since I have left the group but Raju Bhai is still one of my well wishers even today, farther I presume that if I were to meet Shri O.P. Munjal saheb unexpectedly to day I am sure he will first hug me and then perhaps jokingly ask me as to where I had disappeared for all these years?

A sincere salute goes out from the bottom of my heart to all such great personalities with whom I had the good fortune to work with in the Hero group of companies.

AN UNSUNG HARMONY (IN '02 GUJARAT)

A true story of a silver lining in the dark clouds and also perhaps and opportunity squandered by all in high places to bridge the deep communal divide that exists in the Ahmedabad and Gujarat even today, besides an exemplanary story of how the Hindu Bharvad community consisting of some 200 persons, 40 houses 200 cattle cows / buffaloes was totally protected by Muslim family with his clan in a predominant Muslim Juhapura area during the Godhra riots of 02 in Gujarat.

Mirza Riyasat Ali Mughal of Income-Tax and his wife Shermen Mughal a Sr. Officer of A.G. Office possessed a bungalow in the neo rich Prachina Society of Juhapura since the last 5 years, just across the small road opposite was the sprawling Bharvad Vas from times unknown. It is but natural for humans to build relations and the Mughals being very friendly soon became the advisors and well wishers of this innocent lot of Milkmen supplying milk to many a home in Juhapura.

As time went on in the last 5 years a couple of communal flare ups did occur but the Mughals were always there to assure the Bharvads of their safety come what may at their Vas surrounded by the fastest growing ghetto in Asia - namely Juhapura ..

However, this time after the BLOODY 28th Feb when the Hindus lost all sense of Humanity the Bharvad staying here at Juhapura naturally panicked under fear of facing a similar wrought of Muslims Nevertheless, continuously for 4 days & nights. R.M. Mughal saheb his son/nephews and youngsters of close relations plus those connected with us kept constant guard for the well being of the Bharvads and saw to it that no Muslim of Juhapura breach the trust and faith they had imposed in us. Every phone of their anxious relatives at P.P. no of Mughals was duly passed on to the concerned person just to assure their relations out side of this area that they are all safe and secure in the heart of a muslim area.

On the night of 2nd of March of 2002 i.e. the 3rd day of the riots when I was taking a round of my area with a Lawyer friend we were invited for a cup of tea by a group 20 youngster sitting in a group describing the Havoc and misery faced by Muslims all over in Gujarat on that particular day, just then one of them questioned my lawyer friend about our own people keeping a vigil and protecting the Bharvad Vas in Juhapura, were as thousands of Muslims were being burnt alive alongwith property and houses.. gutted to ashes in these riots, should we not ask them to at least leave our area said one? but another hardliner wanted to behave in a similar manner to the treatment being dished out to muslims living in pockets surrounded by hindu dweelings, My lawyer friend pointed at me and told the agitated lot "talk to Mehdi Saheb as the guardian of Bharvads happens to be his Brother-in-Law and close family, sons and nephews. Probably all the youngsters in the family are of your age ! hence, suddenly I was propelled into a very difficult situation surrounded by enraged Muslim youngsters wanting to avenge the needless killings of their Community members taking place all around Gujarat? !?!

Being conered I had very little time to ponder over an answer which would pacify them at the same time make them see reason. Hence, I got up and gazed at the questioning youngsters asking them just 2 simple questions, for I knew that I had to satisfy and pacify them on immediately religious sentiments.

1. What have those achieved by killing Muslims and burning their properties?
2. Do the principal of Islam permit a true musalman / believer of Islam to behave in similar manner with innocent people? no matter what or which community they belong or what religion they profess??

If any one of you has a convincing reply I will my self come down and ask Mughal Bhai my Brother-in-Law to withdraw the protection this very moment, this made each hyper agitated youngster think for a while.... and perhaps realize the futility of it all in fact they realized their folly and from then on it was only protection which the Bharvads got from us and from this part of Juhapura while the rest of Ahmedabad was still burning, yes,, Juhapura called by many a mini Pakistan in Ahmedabad or the hub of muslim evil as perceived by other bhakts!

Two days later this Mukhi came down with a couple of Army trucks & Jawans and picket up the whole Bharvad community lock, stock & barrel away from this place without even a sight scratch on anyone of them or their properties and even their cattle, The farewell was so quite touching when most of them fell at the feet of the Mughals with tears in their eyes blessing and praying for their well beings as they were totally protected in the darkest nights we have ever seen on the soil of Ahmedabad...

On the banks of the river Sabarmati where Gandhiji preached the lessons of non-violence and communal harmony ?

Never-the-less, detailing this incident I had sent a letter to the TOI Ahmedabad immediately about this act of bravery by our family, however a couple of weeks later not a very prominent article was published by this very news paper passing on all the credit of protecting the Bharvad's in Juhapura to some local politician of the area, now that is Politics even in a strife torn Ahmedabad of Godhra Riots !

PS – this fact can be ascertained anytime by sending your reporters was the highlighted line written by me to the TOI Ahmedabad then and the challenge to deny this act of bravely is open to all even today.

REGISTERATION OF A STOLEN BYKE ?

From December 1997 to April 2006 I worked as a Branch Manager of Cama Motors (a prestigious name in the Automobile dealers of Gujarat) at Gandhinagar, here I was assigned the task of looking after the Bajaj Auto and Hindustan Motors Dealerships besides Gandhinagar being outside the Octroi limits of Ahmedabad   all vehicles purchased by Cama motors would land up at Gandhinagar for being unloaded and a througher predelivery checkup adhered to of all Cama dealership vehicles which even included cars such as Mercedez benz, Skoda, Lancer Mitsubushi and Ambassadors cars of Hindustan Motors Ltd.

This period gave me a tremendous experience of Man-management as I had a total staff or over 40 personnel in the Bajaj dealership and just a little less numbers at the car dealerships and was forced, to literary divide my time fruitfully to do justice to both these assignments .

This period saw me shunting daily up and down religiously between Ahmedabad and Gandhinagar for a period which stretched for well over 7 years which was more of an exercise to repair the loss I had incurred in trying to run a 'Hero Motors" dealership at Ahmedabad in a partnership in which I had stacked all my savings and had to close down as it was not viable after a period of 18 months, resigning from the partnership I was handed over a cheque of some Rs 22000/- all that was left from all my investments I had made as a 20% partner who had no choice but to resign from the partnership bearing my share of the losses which brought me close to a very precarious position in life with hardly any savings, no job or a business to earn my lively hood from and a family to support plus run my domestic household.

In such a situation, I mailed a few letters to leading Automobile companies and dealers requesting them to engage me in their services as I was desperately looking for a job, as luck would have it ,I received a call from Cama Motors to come down and meet their CEO Shri S R Diwanjisaheb with whom I had interacted as a Manager from the principal company in my earlier assignment of Gujarat Narmada Auto Ltd.

Shri Diwanji Saheb was aware of my experience and he spent some time in learning my reason for seeking a job the next day he called me to meet Shri Jehangir Cama the chairman of the company and soon I was offered a position to take charge of the Gandhinagar Branch of Cama motors at my earliest convenience.

At Gandhinagar I had the dual responsibility a Managing the Bajaj dealership at Sector 21 at the same taking care of the HM's cars dealership workshop at sector 28 and the PRICE of other Dealerships of Mercedes, Skoda Lancer etc....

`Slowly but gradually I started my fresh innings as a dealer Manager quite cautiously and my hard work started paying dividents at both the outlets, never the less it was during these years that Bajaj Auto started becoming very aggressive in the two wheeler motorcycle marked switching very conveniently from the largest manufacture of scooters in the world to the second largest manufacturer of motorcycles in the Indian two wheeler market. This aggressive stance was passed on to all the dealers who had to promote these directives of the principals and achieve the targets .....a huge Sales field force needed to be recruited and supervised on day to day basis at the Cama Motors Gandhinagar dealership.

In the course of this requirement we happened to recruit a few welleducated local boys from Gandhinagar town specially to penerate the Rural market in the District and to promote Loan finance purchase of the Motorcycles in the smaller towns surrounding Gandhinagar, one such fresh recruit happened to be the son of a Section officer working in one of the State government office his elder brother was employed as a Marketing executive in a leading pharmaceutical company of Gujarat, hence this back ground seemed good enough for me to offer him a Sales trainee position along with many other boys in our dealership besides his looks were quite simple exhibiting no traces of a cunning mind working within it.

During the course of this sales trainee tenure, as usual during the Diwali festival (season) a record sales of

Motorcycles took place, and one customer who had bought a new Pulsar motorcycle just a day previous to Diwali informed me about his new byke being stolen at night from the compound of his residential quarters for which he had registered a police complaint and wanted some other papers as proof of purchase from our dealership for submission to the police station…   As is normally done I was sympathetic towards his loss and asked my assistants to provide him the necessary documents immediately.

Now this incident of the bike being stolen took place somewhere in October 2004 and we had forgotten the whole issue quiet honestly after a couple of weeks, however somewhere in February 2005 the Sales Manager at our dealership Dharmesh Trivedi phoned me one fine evening whilst I was attending work at sector 28 office asking me to come back to the Bajaj dealership at Sector 21 to attend to a matter of urgent importance……I immediately packed my office bag and rushed back to sector 21 anxious and wandering about the reason for such a call.

On getting back to my cabin in sector 21 the RTO agent of the dealership came in with a set of papers indicating registration of a ":Pulser" motocycle bought from Cama motors Pvt. Ltd. on the name and address of our Sales trainee's but as this byke had already been submitted for registration earlier at Diwali and stolen that night its details of Engine no. and chassis no. sale letter etcetra were stored in the memory of the computer records of RTO Gandhinagar which was not accepting the fresh registration of the same byke submitted just recently by our simple but cunning Sales trainee.

Analysing and accessing the whole issue it because quite evident that the byke was stolen by this person and foolishly submitted for RE registration at the same RTO office! On studing the documents submitted I was shocked to note the invoice and Sale letter which only I as Branch Manager was authorized to sign forged with MY signature, hence it became clear that since he had access to the letter heads of the company he had prepared the bill and Sale letter trying to register the stolen byke by forgoing my signature. I then called the Sales manager and the accused Sales trainee into my cabin and questioned him about the byke purchased by him who at first refused to own up the theft but later admitted to commiting it under threat of beeing handed over to the police, his father a Section officer working in the Government sachivalaya was also called and informed about his son's misdeeds and was given friendly advice to meet the original owner who happened to be his neighbor explain (to him) how his son had lifted the byke for fun rides and learning about his mistake wanted, to make amends by returning it gracefully this advice was not followed.... instead the stolen byke was very quictely left in the compound of the original owner in the dead of the night.

Next morning the original owner woke up and was pleasantly surprised to see his stolen byke parked from where it was lifted, promptly rang up the police and asked them to come down for a punchnama a formality required for acquiring back the stolen byke through the police department.

We too rang up the original owner and told him we had information about his stolen byke to which he replied I saw it parked at the same place from where it was stolen and the police have not taken possession of it as yet ! It was alas too late had his father met the neighbour and explained his son mistake the Sales trainee along with gang may not have landed up in jail for trying to 'Register a stolen byke!'.

AN ESCAPE FROM THE MUMBAI DELUGE

In July 2005 I had casually written a letter to Vanaaz Engineering Pune expressing interest in promoting the sale of their CNG conversion kits for 3 wheelers mainly for Bajaj auto rickshaw in Gujarat through Mehdi Motors A proprietory Authorised outlet started by us to settle my son after his graduation this proposal landed up with one of the senior managers of the company who called me over for a discussions at their registered office cum plant at Pune.

July in India is generally the month when most of the schools reopen after summer vacations and railway reservations to and from Mumbai are easy to get hence, I booked my railway ticket to Mumbai but planned a Bus journey from Dadar to Pune to attend the meeting and rush back to Mumbai that very evening and catch the train back to Ahmedabad thereby making it possible to attend office as usual with just a days of casual leave.

All worked as planned, I left for Mumbai in the Gujarat mail on 24th July 2005 on reaching Dadar I crossed over the eastern-side and took an Asiad Bus for Pune, It was certainly a pleasant morning and the rain gods had started to bless the city in short bursts . The bus to Pune left as scheduled and as we started moving towards our destination the rains started increasing infact by the time we reached Pune a number of roads at the enterance of the city were flooded but as the bus we were travelling by being a Volvo and extra tall in height from the ground we managed to clear the flooded roads and reach the destination at Pune.

Getting down here I was greeted with a heavy down pour, never the less I scrambled to a Auto rickshaw standing at the Taxi stand and instructed the cab driver to reach me to the office of Vanaaz Engineering all throughout this local journey in the city of Pune there was no let up in/by the rains.

Having reached Vanaaz I heaved a sigh of relief but to my utter disappointment the senior manager who had called me had instead gone down to Mumbai for some urgent assignment. However, I was asked to spend time with some other official with whom I had more of one sided interaction and promptly left the office after lunch as the thought of reaching Mumbai and catching the train back home was foremost on my mind.

It was around 4 pm that once again the Volvo Bus from Pune left for Mumbai, all was well but the rains on the ways back just wouldn't stop instead seemed heavier on the way back to Bombay infact a traffic jam of some sort started building up from Vashi onwards and by the time we crossed the New Mumbai bridge and reached Chembur we were in the midst of one of the longest traffic jams I have come across, soon it was 8 O'Clock then9 and 10 O'Clock and we may have moved just a couple of Kms in last 3 hours, I knew I had missed my train back to Ahmedabad by then, but the rains were refusing to lament on looking out of the windows one could only see the water level rising on both sides of the roads and endless ques of vehicles in all directions, The mobile phone I was carrying stopped working and we were as if confined to the premises of the bus, a number of local passengers got down and waded their way out through waist deep water but I thought it better to stay put in the bus alongwith some 15 passengers who probably had their homes far off from Chembur where the Volvo had ultimately stopped.

Some co-passengers had their mobiles working and kept on talking to their relatives on and off others called it a day and passed off after uttering the choicest abuses. I too had no choice but to lie low until morning and spent the night dozing on and off getting up looking around and on finding no change in or the situation dropped off to sleep again, indeed this was perhaps the biggest cloud burst which refused to stop and kept pouring cats and dogs through out the night. Having passed the last 12 hours in this pathetic condition I finally made up my mind to collect my over nighter bag and find my way out on foot, hence it was around 8 in the morning that I left the bus waded ahead to a four road junction and asked some local stand byes to direct me towards Dadar which they did. ...there after I may have kept on walking for almost 3 hours through waist deep water when I eventually reached the eastern side of Dadar train terminium as it is still referred to.

This journey and the scenes I came across can undoubtedly be claimed to be the worst I have seen in a natural calamity! Countless of people were wading through waist deep water with carcaasses of animals floating all round one dead corpes was also seen floating in a far off corner of the street, most of the cars parked on the roads lay drowned in hood deep waters and I can remember only chaos and water water every where, people petrified at this site of Mumbai the city loved and where I had spent the most unforgettable years of my childhood and adolescent. I just wanted to get away from it for honestly I could not digest the havoc and destruction caused by the deluge of the unending rains.

Atlast, I managed to reach close to the Dadar central station and wanted at first to phone my wife and son so as to inform them about my where abouts, finally I spotted a STD booth which fortunately was functioning and had a long que in waiting wanting to call their near and dear ones like me and inform them of their well being. It was around 1 pm in that afternoon when I spoke to my wife and assured her that I was alive and would make all efforts to reach back as soon as possible.

On entering the suburbain railway station it was obvious that all trains were cancelled as the tracks were covered with water which was flowing on to the platforms from the tracks below I then crossed over to the western side of Dadar platform and managed to spot a taxi standing opposite the old Kohinoor cinema on approaching it I was pleased to find an old muslim taxi driver siting in it. I talked to him in the Mumbai muslim accent and he agreed to drive me to Mumbai Central railway station through the slush and water we managed to pass Worli and approached Mahalaxmi when he asked me how do you we reach Mumbai Central now? I answered through Gwalior tank Nana chowk to which he replied that I was definitely well acquainted with the city, yes, I replied from the age of 6 to the age of 23 the best years of my life I have lived in this city of dreams and am utterly shattered to find it in such a mess chacha!

Some how we reached Mumbai central station around 2 pm and was disillusioned to learn that all trains leaving Mumbai central stood cancelled as the suburban tracks were flooded, however one railway inquiry personnel informed me that the local trains from Bandra to Borivali have just resumed service and may be if I reach there I may find some other trains for Gujarat from there.

Now that was enough to trigger me to catch a BEST bus back to Bandra which had started plying from Fort to Andheri Via Mahalaxmi, some how I managed to catch this bus and it took me another 2 hours to reach Bandra. At Bandra all the platforms were so crowded that the Police were announcing on the megaphones not to enter the station which may cause a stampede but I took the risk and eventually got into a train from Bandra to Borivali we were packed like sardines but I some how managed to cross this hurdle landed at Borivali then took another shuttle to Dhanu road during the course of this journey I had made friends with one Chacha who was going back to Surat and another young man going back to Ahmedabad who kept on calling me Vakil saheb as I was still wearing a white shirt and the lucky black pant which I generally wear for an interview.

We reached Dhanu road at around 11 in the night and at first had some snacks we then went out to find out any other means of reaching some destination in Gujarat by road but it seemed all the roads were also flooded and jammed with vehicles, hence could take only the rail route to get back just then we saw a few persons approach the Station masters cabin we too went there and were pleasantly surprised to learn that one super fast train to Amritsar from Bandra would stop at this station on a special request, hence all desirous of boarding it should buy their tickets which we immediately complied to for that was the only route left to get back......After a lot of anxious waiting the train finally arrived at around 1 am and we made a desperate effort to get into the General compartment as all the other coaches were locked from the inside and no one was willing to open the doors, never the less this compartment was also jam packed and were let in only after numerous request to those already standing at the entrance having managed an entry we stood all through the journey like sheep hearded in a den. Thank God the train was a superfast and some how we managed to keep standing and not collapse until it reached Baroda at 5:30 in the morning…………

As soon as the train touched the platform, made a DESPERATE effort to push my way towards the exit got out from the station and hastened towards the Bus depot to catch the first bus back home i.e. Ahmedabad, as my body fatique was now telling on me having been on my feet from 8 am of the previous day after deserting the unfortunate Volvo bus from Pune which had become static in the unimagined floods and traffic jam at Chembur, walking through waist deep filthy water from Chembur to Dadar, reaching Mumbai Central station then back to Bandra then to Borivali and then at last to Dhanu Road and finally reaching Baroda at 5:30 am, seeing a good part of the effect and havoc of the Famous Mumbai Deluge with my naked eyes which even a Mumbaiker may not seen or experienced in person.

On entering the Baroda bus depot an intercity bus was about to leave for Ahmedabad which I Just managed to hop on to bought my ticket and fell on to a seat like a heap in a gunny bag! It was raining still even at Baroda and throughout the journey back to Ahmedabad the Express highway was split in part at a couple of places due to the constant down pour which had lashed Gujarat too over the last 36 hours, perhaps not as severely as witnessed (by me) on the way back from Pune and on the night in the Volvo bus at Bombay / Mumbai.

The GSRTC bus reached Ahmedabad at 8 in the morning and was home around 8:30 am and the first think I did was honestly thank God Almighty for giving me the latent energy and courage to fight my way back home through the now acclaimed historic Mumbai deluge and safely reach my family at Ahmedabad. This too was perhaps one of the most unfortable trips undertaken by me in my long years of association of being a travelling SALES MAN though reaching positions of a Regional Manager or General Manager in the course of my professional career or throughout my working career.

MAN PROPOSES GOD DISPOSES

By February 2006 it had become quite evident that Baja auto would withdraw the dealership from Cama motors at Gandhinagar and we may have to call it a day by the end of the financial year i.e. March 2006, hence I started searching urnestly for an alternative for I thought it is better to resign gracefully rather then be asked to leave.

In the prevailing scenario the Bhavnagar Maruti dealer Eternal motors advertised for an opening of a General Manager position against which I put in an application was promptly called for an interview on a Sunday short listed than a final round with the Maruti Regional office at Ahmedbad and the offer letter was formally given to me asking me to join from the first of April 2006 but as I had to give my current employers a month's notice I streched my joining to first of May 2006.

All seemed well infact I had expressed my thanks to the Almighty whenever I said my prayers for keeping my head high in the form of giving a very respectable and decent alternative.

Being out of practice I had forgotten how to operate the computer hence I joined a crash programmed course just go get In touch with computer systems as Maruti dealerships are attached to their HO on an online bases for all kinds of dealings and it would be required of me as a General Manage to communicate with them on the net on daily bases through the computer system.

The day finally arrived and I left my home with my bags for Bhavnagar with my son coming to see me off at the Paldi bus station to board the 7 am Tanna travels bus which reaches Bhavnagar at 10:30 just in time to report for duty on day one of the new job.

As expected I reached the office well in time to join a meeting being conducted by the proprietor of the Dealership for the sales team. The senior officials of the Dealership were present at this meeting and were cordially introduced….. and the day passed off quite pleasantly. However on inquiring with the personal Managers about my residential accommodation which was to be provided by them I was shown a place which was on the verge of being vacated though quite close to the show room and office this place did not give ma a pleasant feeling on visiting it the first time, infact staying alone on the first floor of an unknown city and a secluded place rang a bell of caution in my mind, hence I told the MD of Eternal Motors that I wouldn't mind sharing the place with their Works manager who too was newly appointment as that would give me some company after office hours and a sense of security.

That evening I checked into a newly opened hotel a Bhavnagar and since I had got up early in the morning to report in time on my first day of work I felt exhausted and dropped off to sleep quite easily. The second day of work saw my working table being placed out side the owners cabin on the first floor office premises now this sitting accommodation was a come down from the cabin facilities I was provided at Cama motors, though not pleased I swallowed this placement without a grude and pursued once again the prime task of locating a decent dwelling place and going through the history of Eternal Motors and its modis operandi of running the setup efficiently including the administration of the dealership.

Slowly but gradually I started to gather all the strings of the dealership and even visited the work-shop which was quite huge and well equipped but not systematic. They had even developed a True value outlet close to the main dealership mainly a big room with a tin covered roof the heat in which was unbearable making me wonder, how could one pass the whole of summer here? With the mercury around 40"c in the first week of May, the exercise of searching for a suitable accommodation and spending the night at the hotel went on for 4 complete days and on 5th day by evening I developed a severe stomach ache so on the way back to the hotel I dropped down at a consulting physician known to Eternal motors and got myself examined after which the Doctor presented me a long list of medicines to be taken as he diagnosed some intestinal infection.

That night I had very little to eat in the form of a dinner and tried to go to bed early but could not as I kept on feeling very uneasy and then the ballon burst with visits to the Toilet from midnight to 5 in the morning ! I may have visited the wash room a good 22 or 23 times which reminded me of a Hindi movie in which Amir Khan sprinkles the food of Salman Khan with a laxative powder for Horses famously called "Jamalgota" and poor chap keeps on visiting the loogh/ toilet umpteen times his physical appearance falling from a suited and booted one to torn and tatered fellow barely about to carry himself ?

However, as luck would have it after 5 in the morning the commotion in the stomach stopped by itself and consequently my visits to the toilet too thus stopped, I bid my time till 7 in the morning and rangup my family Doctor on his mobile and narrated to him the whole episode of the previous night, he than asked me if I was in a position to travel to which I answered in the affirmative, he immediately advised me to take the first bus home from Bhavnagar and report directly at his clinic, soon I followed his instructions packed my belongings reached the Bus stop at Bhavnagar and hopped on to the 8 am bus back to Ahmedabad recollecting on the way the last night's horrofic experience !

On safely reaching Ahmedabad I called my son to come and pick me up at the Sarkhej stand from where we went start to my Doctor who daigonized my illness to a severe attack of a Gastro intestinal virus which if not controlled could lead to dehydration and several other complications ahead. He wanted to admit me and put me on a drip but I requested him to allow me oral treatment instead to which he reluctantly agreed provided I took complete bed rest at home for the next 2 days.

Atlast on reaching home both my wife and son gave me their piece of mind advicing me to stop adventurism and to look for a job in and around Ahmedabad where one has easy excess to home made hygenic food and clean drinking water and the close ones to take of you in times of such adversities. After the 2 days of complete rest I promptly rangup the proprietor of Eternal motors and apologized to him for beating a hasty retreat at the same time informing him about my family not being in favour of my working at a place far away from home. He was an understanding person and soon agreed to relieve me from my responsibilities at the dealership, however for me this was yet again the loss of a great opportunity which had come my way but here again (I will have to repeat that) what is destined cannot be waived/changed. Thus the saying may will apply to the 5 day stint at Bhavnagar "Man proposes (but) God desposes".

A GIFT FROM MAULA ALI

My daughter Muhashara had come down all the way from London to give birth to her first baby, it is generally a custom in Gujarat for the daughter to go to her parents home known as "maika" for this purpose and we were eager to fulfill this custom and eager still awaited the return of our daughter.

Soon the day on which our daughter arrived back dawned and after setting for a couple of days my wife Nishat took her for a status checkup to one of the best Gynecologist in our vicinity namely Dr. Mrs Munshi though she was progressing quite well she had to go through some similar tests adviced by the Lady doctor here which she had already taken in London, nevertheless, all extra care and precautions were being taken as the due date kept advancing or drawing closer....in between a big event in the family the marriage of Gulrej Ali Mirza alias Pashu our nephew was celebrated with a lot of fanfare getting his bride from Nasikh even my son in law came down all the way from London just to attend the marriage and went back after a short stay of just 10 days however Dr. Mrs, Munshi was apprehending some problem at the time of delivery and had naturally prepared us for if need be a caesarian delivery...,.   However, my sister-in-law Shaheda dropped in one day in between and spoke well about the facilities available at EKRA Hospital just across the road to our residence on Sarkhej road and convinced Mubashara to registered for a delivery at this hospital perhaps wanting us to avoid the hassle of stretching all the way up to Paldi at the Dr. Munshi's Maternity Home.

The delivery date indicated was any day on or after 20th Dec. but as there was no real signs of any labour pain during this period at last on the 22nd morning my daughter got her self admitted and went through some or deal of a forced delivery because of which complications developed and the Dr's here at EKRA were forced into an urgent decision for a caesarian delivery as the baby in the womb had swallowed some liquid was very harmful to her lungs and in the process hindered her breathing system/ process .

On learning about this Mess on phone I immediately rushed from my office to the hospital and found my wife and son along with the other family members all in panic, when I saw the baby for the first time she was already put on an oxygen support for breathing this was right from the time she was born , perhaps?

All the happiness of becoming a grandfather just vanished in a second and we were soon on our way to probably one of the best infant hospital as it may be in Ahmedabad. the Dr's here were also visiting faculty at reknown hospitals such as Steerling and Appolo and within hours of the child being admitted she was put on a ventilator. The Dr's gives us an ultimatum that the 1st

72 hours were going to be very crucial for her survival and all will depend on how she reacts during this period in fact the 1st 12 hours we were asked to keep our fingers crossed and pray to God to take her though to this period.

That night,   Jehangir and myself hardly slept and we kept on praying to the Almighty GOD to spare our child all difficulties and spiritually entrusted her to the custody of our Imam Maula Ali (A.S). The first critical night passed out without any major problem and so our hopes and aspirations became alive and were encouraged to go to any extent i.e…. to get our child back hail and hearty, her father Hasan (My son in law) was informed about it in London and it was very difficult to assure him that all will be well but since he was associated with the Medical profession he well knew how serious the case was, hence he expressed a desire to Rush down to A'bad from London but we kept on convincing him that we were doing all that should be required and that he could have done had he been here with all the prayers and good wishes at last the worst was over and after the 6th day the Doctors started assuring us that her recovery process towards normalization was progressing satisfactorily.. on the 6th day from birth it is customary to name the baby/ child the name is generally suggested by the child's paternal Aunty but as she was far away in Jhansi I suggested to name the baby as Alishah as we had entrusted her in the supreme care of Maula Ali who was   her

SAVIOUR, Jehangir (Baba) gave her the middle name Batul there by adding to the naming ceremony hence the baby was named AlishahBatul Hasan (Hasan being her family name) slowly but surely Alishah kept on a ventilator surpassed all expectations and came out as a winner, she was finally discharged from the hospital after a period of some 14 days which can be easily called one of the most happiest moments of our lives.

The Doctor's attending on her accepted the fact that even as a new born baby Alishah was a great fighter, hence she retrieved herself from a close call, and I believe that this quality she has in inherited from her parents who have been very persevering and hardworking in wanting to achieve just a little more then what is expected of them in life.

I am quite sure Alisha one day will go a long way and will achieve exceptional heights which will make us all proud …we believe she is a gift to our family from Maula Ali. Nevertheless, the other plus point which this period of crisis brought out was the mature display of attitude and role played by Jehangir for earing to fulfill the smallest requirement asked for by the hospital in the treatment of our baby, keeping in constant touch with the Doctors and nurses attending on her assuring his sister and mother that all was progressing well and giving us the hope that the baby will be well soon with us hail and healthy. When that day really arrived he looked happier than the happiest amongst us.

ADVERSITY AN ADVANTAGE !

It all started with our decision to close down Mehdi Motors….a Bajaj Authorized sales and service point on Sarkhej Road managed and operated by my son Jehangir who was very keen to venture into his own business after completing his graduation as he believed that from a small beginning he had the business acumen to build a flourishing dealership, and establish a family business, as our earlier venture had failed under my command, perhaps ?

However, I thought of taking a chance once again after the loss suffered at Balaji motors by investing a reasonable amount of some 2.5 to 3 Lacks to setup a small business for my son who may just make it big from this humble beginning.

Initially his interest and handwork started paying good results as he had soon picked up the tricks of the Automobile trade and was earning enough to pay for the running expenses of the setup At this juncture we also though of searching for a suitable match for him from our own community and soon we found one from Indore with an informal understanding perhaps ?

The next period of a year and a half was I suppose the most comfortable one in my son's life for soon umpteen hardships were staring him in the face waiting to make' his life quite

miserable. Later on !'

The resignation of Cama Motors from the main dealership of Bajaj Auto which

was handled by me cast its shadow on the mini - Authorized set up of my son as Bajaj were unhappy with anything connected with Cama Motors and their Manager A.G Mehdi and company so they appointed a new outlet in the vicinity of 2 Kilometers from our Authorized outlet at Sarkhej and ordered the main Dealer Popular Automobile at A'bad to stop supply of vehicles for sale to Mehdi Motors.

This was a setback to the smooth growing business cultivated by us, however, we managed to continue on the strength of our Service earnings for a couple of months but as customers closer home started getting the same facilities for their vehicles at their door step, reporting even at the workshop started falling so much so that we had to shell out Rs 8000 to 10,000/pm of our own to keep the setup running. One fine day Jehangir himself along with his mother arrived at a decision to close down the business (though with a heavy heart)

This episode definitely gave a good jolt to my son which set him seriously thinking and hunting for a job, with his experience of a couple of years in selling Automobile vehicles…. he was soon shortlisted for a Mercedes Benz dealership at Bahrain in Gulf for the post of a Sales Executive called for a couple of interviews at Baroda ·and Bombay and was finally selected and sent an Appointment letter by the recruiting agency Bombay but his work Visa was not approved just because our surname happened to be Mehdi, Some extremist outfit with a similar Name in that region which was a sheer coincidence but detrimental to him, now this setback was to hard for JAM as we fondly address him at home and I cannot forget the way he broke down and cried when he was informed that his work permit was refused and the agency had no other option but to send some other candidate in his place.

With this yet another setback we all were naturally very disturbed and my wife could not help but inform my daughter and son-in-law who were in London of this cruel act of destiny..

 In fact which had nothing but prolonged their brother's struggle in life, being equally hurt and disturbed about it they tried to console us and soon reverted to call him to U.K. to pursue further studies with a part time job to enable him to stay of his own and also pay for his educational expenses.

Soon the focus now shifted to making an all out effort to send him to London, hence he first joined an institute preparing students for the IELTS exams a precondition for entry to a U.K. college on a student Visa, since his Medium of instruction in school and college was

English it was not very difficult for him to clear IELTS test in first attempt, pursuant to which my son-in-law Hasan(who played a part more of an elder brother in this crisis) Soon got his admission in a good college at London and we were now in the process of completing his papers for a student Visa to U.K.

In this exercise we wanted to be perfect and here my brother-in-law Mr. Mughal saheb and his wife that is Baba's Mamahuzoor and Mamihuzoor extended their full hearted support by standing by us at this hour of need as his co sponsors offering their house, bank balances and shares to pledge as financial backup along with ours to fulfill the minimum requirement of the norms desired by the U.K. embassy for granting student Visa permit to an individual infact the total financial assets pledged in his students Visa application amounted to over 70 lacks besides giving a number of affidavits and documents bank statements fulfilling the norms! All this and with help of the Almighty God Jehangir was able to obtain his student Visa. this exceptional act of kindness by my laws will never be forgotten and we pray to Allah for their welfare & well being always.

Soon on submitting the papers to the UK embassy Branch at Ahemdabad A Permit to stay and study in U.K. for over 2 years was granted to my son. BY the Bombay British consulate

No sooner had we received his Visa and Passport through the courier his eyes sparkled and lighted up with joy and we all heaved a sigh of relief, he then rang up his sister and brother in law in London who were equally instrumental in this group success story as they had sponsored his accommodation in U.K. he then asked them if he could come down by the next available flight to London to which they answered in the affirmative.

We then rang up all our relatives and in particular his Mamuhuzoor Mughal Saheb and thanked them profusely for all the help which was certainly instrumental in seeing him through. Within 5 days Jehangir Mehdi had left for London after receiving his Visa and his mother (my wife) of course could not get over the fact that her son has left us and gone away to London only to return after a couple of year.

The moral of the story is that failures are nothing but stepping stones to success.

Today my wife and myself many a time MISS our children and Grand children but also feel it was necessary for them to face life as it comes and crave a successful future for themselves though far away from us for we believe our Happiness lies in their being Happy. Isn't it ?

Published Letters
Mosquito Menace

TOI Dt 24th Feb., 1988

Sir – The mosquito menace in the Paldi, Vasana, Sarkhej Road belt of Ahmedabad city has reached alarming proportions. Never in my 13 years in this area have I witnessed such monstrous attacks of mosquito mobs no sooner it is dusk.

The people of this area hope the city fathers will soon find a solution to this problem by bringing an end to the health hazard caused by the usage of sewage waters.

Meanwhile, each household whether rich or poor, spends considerably on mosquito killing sprays and repellents. I wish to make an appeal to all concerned in high offices to bring an end to this horror and restore the basic civic right of peaceful sleep to the people of these area.

A.G.MEHDI

Ahmedabad.

Published Letters'
STATUS OF MUSLIMS IN INDIA

T.O.I. Dt 22nd July, 1988.

Sir, - Maulana Wahiduddin Khan's article (American Asians A role July 12) Is definitely thought proviking and should be followed by the Indian minorities especially the Muslim Nevertheless, the case differs in our country. The Muslim minorities in India is quite different from the Asian American as pointed out in the article the Asian American had migrated to America in search of better opportunities, hence it has always been their endeavor to live a peace with their neighbors and divert all their energy and resources to achieving progress. However in case of Indian Muslims who from 10 per cent of the total population it can be categorically said they have not come from a foreign country in search of better opportunities but have lived here for centuries and have actually degenerated over the years after fall of the Mughal empire and further more in the last few years due to superficial   differences and an unnecessary friction which exists   makes it difficult to come across the likes of another Ghalib, Iqbal or Maulana Azad.

Almost 75 to 80 per cent of the Indian Muslims are uneducated or semi-literate or school drop-outs taking generally to the streets and lesser jobs leading a majority of the community to abject poverty It can nevertheless be derived that contrary to the American Asian the socio-economic condition of an average Muslim is getting from bad to worse.

Being an educated Muslim I have vigorously canvassed for the cause of Muslim educating their children. To get out of the vicious circle of poverty and stand out amongst the rest. This to my understanding would require a massive consolidated effort not only from the Government but from all the educated and well off Muslims plus other philanthropic Organizations in the country.

A.G. MEHDI

Ahmedabad.

Published Letters
SEOUL CAPER

T.O.I. Date: 30th Sep. 1988.

Sir, - Have we sent the Indian Team to the 24th Olympics at Seoul just to stand by the road and cheer as the winners to by?

It is a matter of great shame and regret that in the last few days since the Olympics have started not a single medal be it only a bronze. Has come into the Indian kitty !

A country with a population of more than 70 crore people should hang its head in shame ? should we be compared vis-à-vis with china which is maintain its study accumulation of medals by its world class performances at the Seoul Olympics. The Chinese are in no way superior to the Indians as far as physical strength or ability is concerned!

Should we desire to reach Olympic standards as in the case of China or Japan we would then have to seriously plan to catch our sportsmen very young i.e. at a tender age of 5 or 6 years. Besides the whole country's needs to make an effort to achieve this or may be a desperate effort to achieve this goal. We may even have to go to the extent of making physical education a compulsory subject in the primary schools Vigerous efforts should then be made in spotting young talent and sportsmen in all fields.

After spotting the talent , since efforts should be made right from the grass root level in properly grooming it/them into world class, There efforts should not be restricted to a limited sphere or games but should be extended and adopted for all disciplines/events covered by the Olympic authorities.

Its no use building huge stadia and sports-complexes all over the country and exhibiting a desire to host Commonwealth Games, Olypmics, etc. without actually having a breed of world class Indian sportsmen?

A.G. MEHDI

Ahmedabad.

Published Letter
Xenophobia Or Acceptance

My mother, of Iranian origin, came to India at the age of six, grew up, studied and got married to my father, a 'complete' Indian.

The couple were blessed with two sons. In spite of having all her relatives and property in Shiraz (Iran) my mother chose to never go back and settle in the land of her birth. Today after 60 years all she does is to diligently look after my father, an old man of 70 with a fractured hip joint who uses a walker even to move about inside the house. She has stood through it all, and with us, has imbibed all the traits of a true Indian wife and mother.

One can never mistake her as a foreigner except when one carefully listens to her accent. Can any one now distrust her or any one like her just because her origin is foreign?

A.G. Mehdi, Ahmedabad

T.O.I.

Dt. 17/9/99

Published Letters
ON LIFETING OF BAND ON RSS IN GOVT ?

T.O.I. DT. 23/1/2000

As an Indian Muslim, I feel that the RSS consists of shakhas totally dedicated to the well being of the country. Nevertheless, it has been allergic to the growth, and progress of the minorities in India, evidenced by its deeds and actions, from its inceptions which actually tarnishes its credentials, By allowing government employees to participated in activities, I feel, we are just inviting more trouble in the chaotic government structure which is not free from corruption and favoritism. Gujarat is today perceived as communally hyper sensitive state. Permitting employees to join RSS will only widen the communal divide.

A.G. Mehdi, Sarkhej, Ahmedabad.

Published Letters
State Losing Sheen

August, 2000

The Gujarat *Bandh* called on Thursday August 3 by the VHP to protest against the killings of Amarnath pilgrims in Jammu Kashmir has succeeded in spreading only violence and hatred in Gujarat which can by far boast to be the most communally sensitive state in the country !

The Bharat Bandh called the next day did not in the least turn violent except for a few stray cases of stone putting and road blockades in some parts of Assam, AP, Maharashtra etc. The communal hatred being pioneered and groomed in the state does not augur well for its development and future and its high time someone takes up the mantle to explain to the majority of the fanatics that the minorities even to day, are the ones who take a leading role in condemning terrorist the killings of innocent pilgrims.

The uncalled for violence against the minorities have marred the success of the cause in Gujarat. On the contrary, it indicated some kind of a sanction from the government and police to turn this tragedy in to a communal issue.

A.G. Mehdi, Ahmedabad

The Editor

2nd Jan 2000

The Times of India,

Ahmedabad – 380009

Dear Sir,

Apropos your front page headlines dtd. 1stJan, 2000 Government Hobsons's choice Firstly gives a very blurred picture of the release drama, besides conveying a weak decision taken by the Government in power in the hijack episode, serious remarks, are ambiguously attributed to "a senior minister" on reasons of release and suggest of the government buckling under pressure and playing into the hand of the Taliban as officials say the settlement was 'forced by the Talibans'.

Secondly, it is shocking to note how the Government arrived at a conclusion that any massacre of a passenger on the plane could trigger off communal riots in the country ? which actually did nor erupt even during the Kargil war lasting for over two months.

Yes, instead we fought shoulder to shoulder at Kargil and spared no words in condemning this dastardly hijack, offering even to go down to Kandhar to negotiate release of hostages with the highjackers. How many are aware of the special prayers offered by so many an Indian Muslim in various mosques after observing 'Roza' the whole day in the evening of 30th December,

1999 begging the Almighty the safe return of the hostages majority of whom were not Muslim but Indian brethren ?

Thanking you,

Yours Truly,

A.G. Mehdi

67, Navrang Society,

Sarkhej Road,

Ahmedabad.

From :-A.G. Mehdi

67, NavrangTenaments,

Sarkhej Road,

Ahmedabad-55.

Date :- 22-9-2000.

To.

The Editor, (Letters Deptt.)

The Times Of India.

Ahmedabad.

Dear Sir,

The New BJP President Shri Bangaru Laxman has Kicked Off A new controversy to woo Muslims to join the Party where as some other members Of the Sangh

Parivar Including many In the BJP it self are quite opposed to it.

After Partition the Indian Muslim have suffered the most including a Cultural Set Back as political parties including the Congress have only used them for political gains leading to a Degeneration and stagnation of the Community and all roads to progress and prosperity are completely blocked, for which even the community itself is also to be blamed !

Today Muslims which form a good 15% of the population of our country is not proportionately represented In The Ministry, Govet. Jobs, Police and other seats of power infact an unwritten understanding exists in all quarters to deny Muslims respectable jobs and positions. In the last 18 years of my career after graduating from Bombay St.Xavier's College with a Management Diploma I have Suffered Denials of equal Opportunity and Promotions And instead received punishment transfers Thank God Presently I am employed in a Parsi Firm which treats all on merit.

Its time the Muslim now awake to the facts and create their Importance In the Country by Educating The Present generation making them eligible for their due share by striving for it and not by being Appeased.

In Conclusion let the BJP know that as of today that their Proposal to woo Muslim seems quite similar to the one being offered by General Musharaf of Pakistan who wants to talk to India for a negotiated settlement of Kashmir without stopping cross border Terrorism.

Regards,

(A.G. Mehdi)

Fax – 6583758

People Power

Dt:- 10/11/2000

Dt:- 20/11/2000

Do you Feel the American Poll Dispute Could Have Been Speedily Resolved It They Could Like India Have A Poll Supervisory Body To Order A Repoll As Suggested By C.E.C. Shri M.S. Gill (?)

Many a Time our Political Pandits Had Second Thoughts About Our Political Form and System Of democracy but the American Poll Dispute For Its Highest Office have made One realize that Yes, India with its Parliamentary form of democracy is by far the best in the world, the commission headed by the CEC Can Order a Repoll against any kind of vote rigging / tempering with ballot papers, boxes or any other fraudulent practices in the process of casting a vote any time any where.

To-day the worlds super power is not even able to declare its most political powerful man since the last three days for its simple lack of not having an arbitery body like the one we posses. Reelections can be ordered in India any time by the election commission be it a part or whole of a constituency, within hours of its ascertaining doubt of a constituency, within hours of its ascertaining doubt of use of fraudulent voting practices.

We as Indians can boast today of our election system and its implementation thereof as the largest democracy of the world religiously following it since last 50 years. Bravo India and its democracy.

(A.G.Mehdi)

From :-

A.G.Mehdi

67, NavrangTenaments,

Sarkhej Road,

Ahmedabad-55.

Published Letters
The Mask

T.O.I. Dt. 13/12/2000

Two statements made by Prime Minister Vajpayee in the last couple of months, first during his US visit of being a "true Swayam Sevak" and the other recently about the temple at Ayodhya being a "unfinished task" has sent shock waves among the Muslim.

Unfortunately, the conceived notional concept of Vajpayee being a moderate, judicious and truly secular government head, despite of his Sangh Parivar links , stands exposed. Almost anyone having little knowledge of law can conclude that the much awaited Supreme Court judgment on Ayodhya is unlikely to favour those who perceived, planned and pulled down the Babri mosque. In such an atmosphere, the PM wants to strike a bargain with the Muslim to obtain the temple.

A.G.Mehdi, Ahmedabad

Date :- 30/01/2001.

To,

The Editor,

Times of India,

Letters Department,

Ahmedabad – 380009.

Sir,

The Natural Furry That struck Gujarat At 8-46 Am In The Form Of A Massive Earthquake On 26th January 2001 And the Aftermath Have Established The Following Facts :=

a) Great Scientists Like Mr. Hawkins Or Computer Wizards Like Bill Gates Cannot Precisely Predict The Exact Time Or Intensity Of A Quake Calamity.

b) That in the eyes of god all humans are equal irrespective of their religion, caste, creed, wealth, nationality etcetera only proving that a super power known as the almighty certainly exists and the wrong doers, should known that the law of nemesis can still prevail.

c) That while earthquakes cannot be controlled the corrupt and malpractices of the ones guilty for inviting death and destruction which could have been avoided can be taken to task.

d) That the help and Aid which will now flow from all over the world for the deserving and needy should be kept away from the greedy hawks and corrupt caretakers lest their presence and interference impedes and diverts aid from the areas really affected and should avail it.

e) That it took a major catastrophe for the communal hatred to be buried for the moment in Ahmedabad and Gujarat and the Hindu and Muslim volunteers held hands in relief work acknowledged by national dailies and T.V. Channels but for the "Local Gujarati D.D." Channel which still PROJECTS the contribution of only a SINGLE community !

Regards

(A.G.Mehdi)

From :-

A.G.Mehdi

67, Navrang Society,

Sarkhej Road,

Ahmedabad 380055

Published Letters
OPINION ON BUILDER'S AFTER GUJARAT QUAKE

T.O.I. Dt 18/2/2001

It's been three weeks since the calamity struck and a handful of builders have been charge-sheeted with promises from high ups in the government to book the errant. Let me remind the government that it has forgotten the officials of its own agencies who have issued OK certificates for occupying these ill-fated building without even probably visiting just to obtain their 'fees'.

The speed with which our judiciary dispenses justice is known to all hence the nexus can take advantages of the public's short memory and within a few months all may be forgotten perhaps even forgiven.

If the government really wants to book the guilty, it should pass an ordinance setting a deadline for prosecution orders within stipulated period of time.

A.G. Mehdi, Sarkhej, Ahmedabad.

Date :- 20th March 2001

The Editor Edit page,

The Times of India,

Ahmedabad- 38009,

Sir,

'Power corrupts, more power corrupts more' no doubt tehelka has dug up the dirt be it the transparency of our democratic system or the slip offered by the guilty bureaucracy / politicians the revelations are certainty shocking enough to make every Indian head hang in shame presumably a national disgrace.

In a similar exposure last year when match fixing scam came to light, those in power were adamant to take back the arjuna awards of the sportsmen Implicated imposing a lifetime ban of the accused. Should not the same norms be applied to those found guilty now ?

In conclusion, I foresee far reaching consequences of this episode which will now further deter, decent, clean and honest persons/citizens to refrain from holding any desire of actively entering the political profession, which is disgraced and carries a stigma. It's a pity to note senior ministers forcing their juniors to take back their resignations just to hold on to power !

Regards

(A.G.Mehdi)

A.G.Mehdi.

67, Navrang society,

Sarkhej road,

Ahmedabad-380055

Published Letters
Crying Foul

T.O.I. Dt 4/5/2001

Apropos the report by your civic reporter about the sewage treatment plant coming up at Juhapura (TOI, April 27). Do you think resident of any area would not raise a hue and cry about the issue when two such plants already exist in close vicinity and two new ones are proposed close to its residential habitat?

But It a "State of Art plant sans the foul smell "isn't it obvious why the area has been singled out for such treatment. Why were the new high Courts or civil hospital building not set up in the area?

I, on behalf of the residents of Juhapura, make a fervent plea to municipal commissioner Kailash Nathan to first upgrade the existing plants so that we human beings are not exposed to the foul odour and pollutions we are suffering at the moment. Besides, since the new STP plants are going to be state – of – part units any other part of the city should have no problem in accommodating them?

A.G. Mehdi, via' e-mail

Published Letters
Only Option

T.O.I. 4/6/2001

A propos the letters by a Mr. Thadhani and H Desai ITOI, May 31). I take opportunity to refute their negative perceptions and complement Prime Minister Vajpayee for the bold step he had once again taken to give peace a chance.

The Kashmir issue has made life miserable not only for Kashmir's but also for the people of India and Pakistan. The wars, cross-border terrorism and mass killings since the last 50 years bear testimony to this fact. In such a situation should not one endeavor to at least take the first step towards inviting peace and tag on a change of attitude ? Yes, the road to peace which will be filled with impediments but the effort certainly cannot be called futile.

Without talks, how else can the problem be solved? The experience of the last 50 years must have convinced both by politicians and extremist elements on both sides of the border that it definitely cannot be solved using force. There is no doubt about the sincerity and honesty of Vajpayee on the matter. Otherwise, he would not have made the journey by bus to Lahore or invited Mushraf for talks.

The ball is now in the General's court and he will have to respond to Vajpayee's gesture by visiting India with an open mind.

A.G.Mehdi,

via e-mail

Date :- 13/7/2001.

To,

The Editor,

People Power,

The Times of India,

Ahmedabad.

Will the Agra summit yield anything concrete results?

Please refer my letter in your daily dated 4th June 2001 in which I have clearly expressed hard talks are the only choice to settle differences between India and Pakistan, the good intentions of Shri Vajpayee are very obvious and clear and that the history of India will remember him as the one who iniciated many a step to create an atmosphere of permanent peace between India and Pakistan.

The Agra summit will yield a concrete result as it will now make known to us the true intentions of president General Musheraf and his colleagues if they are sincere in clearing the atmosphere of mistrust, they will come to Agra with an open mind and a clean slate leaving behind all the past and vice versa if they are not!

Its true the Kashmir issue is the bone of contention between us, but such a hyper sensitive issue cannot be solved in just one or two meetings / summits. It will need a Herculean effort from not only the leaders of both the countries but from the people of India and Pakistan to accept the realities and adust to some give and take in order to arrive at a compromise solution over a period of time. However in the meantime since the people of both the countries share a common history of thousand of years let us come a little closer on other aspects (for the betterment of both) such as trade and commerce technology culture sports etc. and with a little luck from my friends the contentious issue will be resolved in due course of time, Inshallah.

In conclusion, I once again retreat that the ball is not in the Generals court and all depends on how he maneuvers it to yield concert positive results.

A.G. Mehdi

67 NAVRANG SOCITY,

SARKHEJ ROAD,

AHMEDABAD – 380055.

Published Letters
Wrong Stand

T.O.I. Dt 10/09/2001

Isn't it hypocritical for the Government of Indian to shun a discussion on the status of castiesm in India at the UN Conference on Racism in South Africa ? Gandhiji started his crusade against discrimination in South Africa and fought a non-violent war against castiesm. Yet we are wanting to turn a blind eye to the cause for which our leaders stood and preached sermons of equality. I think we have a long way to go as far as human rights, equality and castiesm is concerned.

A.G.MEHDI, Ahmedabad.

Date :- 15/9/2001.

To,

The Edit Page Edition,

The Times of India,

Ahmedabad – 38009.

Dear Sir,

The letter written by Shri PrafullGoradia in your esteemed daily Dt. 14th instant titled the Dividing line sounds quite provocative then sympathetic for hos Muslim brothers in India. May I be permitted to ask, is any Indian Muslim in his individual capacity or an organization associated with the dastardly act committed by who so ever on WTC or pentagon In America ?

A backlash against a particular community is bound to occur when thousands of innocent lives in American or even at the Assignation of charismatic leader in India, but it certainly does not mean all persons belonging to that community are responsible for it ?Infact president Bush has amply made this clear in assuring American Muslims About their safety.

In conclusion . Indian Muslims are in no way connected with the Terrible Tuesday episode and totally condemn it for a true Muslim can never kill innocent people, hence we perceive a very clear line supporting right against a wrong committed and advice out dear friend Goradia not to be unduly disturbed his Muslim brethren in India.

Regards,

(A.G,Mehdi)

67, NAVRANG SOCITY,

SARKHEJ ROAD,

AHMEDABAD.

Date : 21/9/2001.

If terrorist had launched an operation similar to the one on WTC in India would the world have been so concerned?

Certainly not ? Terrorism was never seen in the right perspective until WTC happened. "Only the wearer knows where the shoe pinches?" India had been crying hoarse since the last 10 to 15 years of the havoc terrorism has played with its people initially in Punjab and recently in J&K but its seemed the whole world has turned a blind eye to it. The loss of two of our finest leaders Mrs. Indira Gandhi & Rajiv Gandhiji bear testimony to one of the most dastardly acts of terrorism in this part of the world, yet some of our neighbors called it a freedom struggle sitting in the very luxury of the hospitality offered by us and we stood dumb founded even to verbally refute it!

The attack on WTC in the US is a symbolic attack well planned by the terrorist on the pride and prestige of the mightiest power on earth and now the whole world stood shaken up to the reliasation of terrorism!? those who sweared to the Freedom struggle soon vowed to take the most stringent steps to eliminate it from the face of this earth.

In conclusion, perhaps if WTC would not have happened the world would have realized the Agony we were suffering since so many years ?

A.G. Mehdi

67, Navrang Society,

Sarkhej Road,

Ahmedabad.

Date :- April 22,2004

To,

The NDTV India,

Greater Kailash-I,

New Delhi

Kind Attn: - Shri Rajdeep Sardesai

Dear Sir,

With the completion of polls of the 1st round / Installment of the General Elections to the 14th Lokhsabha the following facts seem abundantly clear from the trends observed in Gujarat.

a) That at least 58% of the population in Gujarat did not buy the "India shinning' concept proposed by BJP or perhaps did not FEEL GOOD enough to cast a vote in its favour ?

b) That only 43% of the total voters cast there vote in the Political Laboratory of the BJP indicating the writing on the wall about its prospects in the future rounds.

c) That the low percentages of voter turnout, in constituencies belonging to National stalwarts are yet another proof of there loss of appeal and credibility.

d) That the Muslims in Gujarat are once again being taken for granted that they will only vote forthe Congress as the party did not even bother to campaign in certain areas (dominated by Muslims populations) where as the BJP totally neglected them on the other hand which is nothing new or surprising as it is a continuous process adopted by the B.J.P. Government, since it's coming to power in the state of Gujarat!

Regards,

A.G.Mehdi

67, Navrang Society,

Sarkhej Road, Ahmedabad-380055.

Letter sent to many T.V. channels and dailies before the 14[th]Lokhsabha Elections.

AN APPEAL TO ALL INDIAN MUSLIMS

In a state like U.P. where the Muslims vote is in sizeable proposition in many pockets their decision to favor a particular candidate can became the turning point of the Election Game.

It's high time the community releases its importance and comes on a single platform not to support a candidate from a particular party but to identify the best consensus secular candidate in their constituency and vote in uniform to enable him to win.

The main goal of Indian Muslims in this General Election should be to promote secularism and to discard communalism even in their own community if such elements are found in and around they should be shunted out and stopped from polluting the society.

Islam has never preached hatred towards any one hence the philosophy of hatred towards any community or person should be totally eliminated

 from the minds of Muslims at large and a desire to live in peace and a pleasant tomorrow should be cultivated.

The united efforts to support the right candidate singularly irrespective of party affiliations will make the majority release the strength of the minority and also the cost of neglecting it.

Let us then try to become the Turning Point of the 14th General Election in India.

19th May, 04

The Editor

The Edit Page

The Times of India

Ahmedabad.

Dear Sir,

Now that the 14th General Elections in the country have peacefully transferred the power to the Congress combination. The following facts need a special point of note :-

a) That the NDA failed to keep the promise it gave and no amount of good Advertisement and publicity can seal a bad proposal or product.

b) That the derogatory Foreign origin campaign pursued by many in the BJP projected it as a party bereft of issue Agenda or Achievements.

c) That the proposal of changing of a Parliamentary system of Election into a Presidential one did not result in helping Atalji win votes.

d) That the last minute appeasement of the Muslims by the BJP without carrying out the Rajdharam on many an occasion received a negative response from the Muslims and turned away a good deal of staunch Hindu supporters.

e) That the Muslims have voted for the Congress at large after 9 years with the hope that they will not be taken for granted as in the past and a lot of wrong done to the community in the last 6 years will be set right.

In conclusion the Congress combination should keep in Mind the often repeated lines of Shri Pandit Jawaharla Nehru while taking charge of the reins of power.

The woods are now going to be dark lonely and Deep ……. and we have miles to go before we sleep.

Regards,

A.G.Mehdi.

A.G.Mehdi

67, Navrang Society

Sarkhej Road,

Ahmedabad – 380055

To,

Letters,

C/o.Edit Page Editor

The Times of India,

Ashram Road,

Ahmedabad – 380009

Sir,

During or after the Agra summit the use of the word "JIHAD" has increased considerably, being a Muslim I will therefore like to clear some doubts in the minds of my nonmuslim friends about its meaning or implication.

I am certainly not a religious scholar but as an average Muslim understands 'Jihad' it means a call for a holy war or struggle given by a religious head to the community to defend the religion or community from being extinguished.

Now, when General Mushraf can call cross Border terrorism as a freedom struggle, why can't the terrorist call their acts of violence in the valley as 'Jihad' – a religious war sans any threat of the religion or community being wiped out (?)

The aggression stepped up by the Fanatical groups after the Agra summit specially the unwarranted killings of Amarnath Pilgrims and the uncalled for massacre of Doda Hindus cannot be termed as freedom struggle or an act of 'Jihad' by not only the Indian Muslim but by any true Muslim on earth.

The General may have changed his tone on Independence Day by saying they will go to any length with India …. But actions against the enemies from within whom I suppose he has finally identified.

Regards,

A.G.Mehdi

67, Navrang Society,

Sarkhej Road,

Ahmedabad – 380055.

8th March, 05

To,

The Editor,

The Edit Page,

The Times of India,

Ahmedabad.

Dear Sir,

Last Sunday, I watched the interview of senator Mrs.Hillary Clinton in the India Today Channel and was highly impressed with the manner in which she exuberated self confidence, she replied each question quite convincingly and spoke on behalf of her country in one voice irrespective of the ideological difference she may have as a democrat senator vis-à-vis the Republicans who hold the present position of power in America.

As against this backdrop in the other hand the programme on NDTV 24/7 conducted by non other than Rajdeep Sardesai my favorite analyst. The Big Fight was nothing but A Big Fight in true sense of the word on the santity of the Governors office in our country it was disheartening to see, the BJP and the CONGRESS debating the status of Governor his Rights / Duties etcetera each one of the speakers were just flinging mud at each other. It was therefore distressing to compare the two programs and suggest that if we in India continue in the same manner we will soon ruin all the progress we have achieved (politically and economically) in the last 50 years.

The logger head attitude adopted by both the main line parties is a matter of serious concern to "We the people of the largest democracy of the world" and its high time senior politicians / leaders of our country confine their differences to ideologies pursued and work in unison to iron out objections amicably, to help make out country a force to reckon with in the International arena.

Regards,

A.G.Mehdi

67, Navrang Society,

B/H Fatehwadi bus stop,

Sarkhej Road,

Ahmedabad – 380055

67, Navrang Society,
B/H Fatehwadi bus Stop,
Sarkhej Road,
Ahmedabad – 380055.
Date :- 06/07/2005

The Edit Page Editor,
The Times of India,
Ahmedabad – 380009.

Dear Sir,

A terrorist is a person who uses extreme means to strike fear in its opponents. He as a rule fights for a cause which is not acceptable by the majority and the means he uses to reach the end are violent and torturous trying to hurt the opponent mentally and physically.

Before entering an extremist organization the person enrolled has to pledge to severe all relations and fight for attainment of the cause at any cost be it his life.

By abiding and following such rules a person automatically ejects himself from being a believer of God or any faith, hence a terrorist should not be identified as member of any community or religion as he GOES AGAINST THE BASIC NORMS of HUMANITY leave alone religious principles.

Regards,

A.G.Mehdi

67, Navrang Society,

B/H Fatehwadi Bus Stop,

Sarkhej Road,

Ahmedabad – 380055.

Date :- 15/06/2005

The Edit Page Editor,

The Times of India,

Ahmedabad – 380009

Sir,

The return of Shri L.K. Adwani from his goodwill Pakistan visit opened up a Pandora box which dug up many a grave of bygone leaders.

After 50 years we are once again debating who was actually responsible for the partition of Akhand Bharat was it the attitude of Muslim League, the RSS the Congress or the Bristishers who took advantage of our hard line attitudes then?

The same tendency exists even today in certain sections and pockets of the entire region (perhaps not satisfied with the price it paid) which can prove to be impediments for bringing about some semblance of unification in the future.

Its for all of us to decide once again whether the future will belong to those who prepare for it or to those who live in the past?

Regards,

A.G.Mehdi

67, Navrang Society,

B/H Fatehwadi bus Stop,

Sarkhej Road,

Ahmedabad – 380055.

Date :- 17/10/2005

To,

The Editor,

The Edit Page,

The Times of India,

Ahmedabad – 380009.

Dear Sir,

When the Congress came to power in the Municipal Elections at Ahmedabad 5 Years ago the BJP had then stood exposed for its numerous acts of commission and omission nevertheless, this time the writing was very much on the wall for the Congress and I am not the least surprised at the pathetic results obtained by them which can be attributed to their own doings :-

1st Lack of proper guidance and planning right from the top central leadership to the lowest in hierchy at Ahmedabad.

2nd Inability to work out a collation with the NCP and SP to avoid loss of votes.

3rd Inability to project their achievement and urge the electorate to give them a 2nd term.

4th Taking the Muslims for granted as a Peggy bank of votes without doing anything for them.

The timing / dates were ill conceived as being conducted in Ramzan many a Muslim was too lethargic to linkup at polling booths, where as the BJP with all its odds and infighting, factionalism urged its voter to cast the mandate.

The Ahmedabad results are a serious warning to the congress to pull up their socks and do something to make their supporters feel that they care, lest it may must be a complete white wash of their power in all local bodies of the hundutava laboratory !

Regards,

A.G. Mehdi

67, Navrang Society,

B/H Fatehwadi bus Stop,

Sarkhej Road,

Ahmedabad – 380055.

3rd Jan 2007

MY TIME MY VOICE

C/o. The Editor Times Nation,

Ashram Road,

Ahmedabad – 380009

Dear Sir,

Reference your front page "India Poised" on the 1st day of 2007 which was undoubtedly written with a good feeling and a positive attitude for the betterment of all us Indians.

We are surely taking big strides in the international arena and building up an impressive performance in all fields their by creating a progressive world image of the country, However a lot still needs to be done at home first" for charity begins at home" and does not end there, problems quite major still lie unresolved such as corruption, communalism, castiesm, poverty, inequality,

Education, Health, Justice and bridging the gap ? All need to be attacked on war footing. All these evils are abundantly obvious in Ahmedabad itself leave alone the other parts of the country?!

An optimist always, I pray to the Almighty God that with your help and endeavors this may defiantly be our year bringing a positive change to every ones lives irrespective of his being a Hindu or a Muslim, Brahmin or a Harijan, Premji or Pauper. Bihari or a Gujarati

, American or an Indian – perhaps then we can really acknowledge and experience the truth of India shining.

Regards,

A.G.Mehdi

A.G.Mehdi

67, Navrang Society

Sarkhej Road,

Ahmedabad – 380055

Shri Vinod Dauji,

NDTV India

Greater Kailash

New Delhi

Dear Sir,

Re. : Hindustan Humara Hai ?

In appreciation of the above mentioned programmed being hosted by you on your prestigious channel which I watch without fail is really educative and introspective.

As an educated Indian Muslim viewing the programme please permit me to express my view on the episode and the reasons for the status of Muslim in the country, over the last two years, it was indeed painful to note that the Muslims in general have hardly made any progress in a country which is making an all out effort to become a global player and later on global power. Even the Middle class Babu, the weaker section and the whole country had made giant strides for a better life style but the Muslims in general are left to languish in ghettos in all major cities of India, most of the viewers opine and rightly so that the community itself is to blamed but is it not the government who so ever in power have hardly done anything in the last 60 Yrs for the community deliberately using it only as a vote Bank ?(as per the Sakar Committee report)

This situation infact has led the extremist elements in the community to mislead the youth by urging them to fight for their rights and survival by adopting the path of destruction and extremism falling easy prey to membership of terrorist organizations wanting to take advantage of this kind of a scenario.

It is humbly suggested that the media should impress upon the government to make a huge effort to win over the community and educate them sufficiently enough to make them broadminded and progressive in fact a legislation making education compulsory for all is the need of the hour rather than reservation for the minorities!.

The MAIN factor responsible For the degeneration of the Muslims is the extremist posture adopted by certain institution of the majority community who are not willing to accept the minorities as equal citizens of the country one often hears comments that they should be packed off to Pakistan....? well if that is the case than the constitution will also have to be altered and the word secular deleted from the constitution of India! how ever on the other hand though Pakistan was formed as an Islamic State and we have hardly heard of minorities being illtreated as much as they are in secular India Today !?!?

Finally living in Gujarat the Muslims, here have become immune to being treated as they are and even if India is drifting away from secularism it will not be difficult for us to accept it willingly which perhaps Muslims in other parts of Bharat may find it a little difficult to accept !

Can we then say with hesitation that KYA HINDUSTAN HAMARA HAI, OR SOME PEOPLE ARE MORE EQUAL THAN OTHERS ! DAUJI.?

Thanking you

Yours an Alert Viewer
A.G.Mehdi

December 10, 2008

To, Editletters@dnaindia.net

Dear Sirs,

The result of the recent state assemble election to, Five states coupled with the latest Mumbai terror attack from across the border have made the following issues amply clear:-

a) That it was biggest bashing to communal politics played in the country since the 90's (perhaps all political parties took advantage of it for their electoral gains).

b) Performance and results by any government or it's leaders is evident and pays, wiping out the anti-incumbency factor of the voters.

c) That the V.I.P. ism of the lords Maharajas and politicians is an adverse factor and will not be sustained in a democratic set up any longer.

d) A wake up call to all Indians to stands as one against all forms of internal and external attacks to divide the country.

e) And finally a warning to the world at large beware of INDIA AS A NATION, enough is enough and no longer threats and attacks on our Equality, Sovereignty and the Democracy of our Republic will be tolerated.

I presume those in power and to even those who aspire to be in power…. should take a leaf from the above lessons the combined events have brought to fore.

Regards,

A.G.Mehdi

67, Navrang Society,

Sarkhej Road,

Ahmedabad- 380055.

Date: January 21, 2009

To. Editletters@dnaindia.net

Dear Sir,

President Obama's Inaugural Speech at the swearing in ceremony contained a line which impressed me most and which had a philosophical meaning "People will remember you on what you can build and not on what you can destroy" These two lines had conveyed a massage to the departing president and also to the world at large what he intends to do, his invitation to the extremists to open their fist and stretch their hand for a reconciliation were also very impressive and deep.

In just 10 minutes he really made one feel this is really a very small world (as the saying goes) besides our political leaders need to take a leaf out of this attitude and get over the petty divides created by them for their personal political gains.

ALL THE BEST MR.PREZ BARACK HUSSEIN OBAMA.

Regards,

A.G. Mehdi

The Royal Highnesses
of Khanibhai,
Pray hark your honour,

A.G. Mehdi
67, Navrang Tenaments, Nr. Khrusheed Park,
Sarkhej Road, Ahmedabad - 380 055
Phone : 8620651226~~~~~~~~

16th. December 2009.

Please permit me to enlighten yourselves, on the enclosed photograph initially clicked perhaps 90+ years ago and has a story to tell as it has passed hands through 5 — generations of my family.

We presume, it was initially gifted as a memoir from a Royal 'Navasa' to his affectionate 'Nana' and also from a prince who was a 'Bhanja' to a proud 'Mamu' who preserved it en our Ancestral house for many a years, subsequently collected by my late father who had nothing but Adulation for the prince en the picture which became a part of the family collection of framed photographs of the Mehdi Family in our present house.

As for myself, I always adored this Royal personality whose blessings helped me achieve a respectible position en life.

Now coming to the present generation, once when my son a few years back came across this photograph and asked me who it belonged to, I briefed him on it and how his Great Grand Father and Great Grand Uncles had to protect the heir Apparent en ascending the Throne of Khanibhat!

The photograph which had Great sentimental value for the late Nana' Ghulam Rasoolmiya and his decendents we have retrieved and enlarged (it) to be presented to the Royal family of Khanibhat once again as a memoir with a request neverthe-less to accept this small gesture now from the family of late Ghulam Mehdimiya.

With humble respects,

Abbas Mehdi (Kazim)

P.S. Request to convey choice of frame which will be complied with, your Highnesses.

www.ingramcontent.com/pod-product-compliance
Lightning Source LLC
La Vergne TN
LVHW041509170726
843492LV00005B/1428

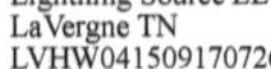